VEGETARIANA

A Rich Harvest of Wit, Lore
and Recipes

VEGETARIANA

A Rich Harvest of Wit, Lore and Recipes

Written and Illustrated by
NAVA ATLAS

The Dial Press
Doubleday & Company, Inc.
Garden City, New York

Text design by Nava Atlas

Library of Congress Cataloging in Publication Data
Atlas, Nava.
Vegetariana.
Includes index.
1. Vegetarian cookery. 2. Vegetarianism. I. Title.
TX837.A85 1984   641.5'636
ISBN 0-385-27910-8
Library of Congress Catalog Number 83-10103

First Edition

In memory of my father

ACKNOWLEDGMENTS

Grateful acknowledgment is given to these publishers and agents for permission to use the following material. Best efforts were made to obtain permissions for use of copyrighted materials from original sources. Please refer any corrections to The Dial Press for future editions.

Crown Publishers, Inc., New York:
From *The New Larousse Gastronomique* ©1977: a quotation on soup by Grimod de la Reynière, reprinted by permission.

J.M. Dent and Sons Ltd., London:
From *The Fables of Aesop and Others* ©1958: a fable entitled "The Fox and the Crow", reprinted by permission.

Doubleday and Co., Inc., New York:
From *The Enlarged Devil's Dictionary* by Ambrose Bierce edited by Ernest J. Hopkins ©1967: a quotation on sauces, reprinted by permission.

E.P. Dutton and Co., Inc., New York:
From *Not That It Matters* by A.A. Milne ©1948: a quotation on potatoes, reprinted by permission.

Harcourt Brace Jovanovich, Inc., New York:
From *Smoke and Steel* by Carl Sandburg ©1920: a poem entitled "Soup", reprinted by permission.

Harvard University Press, Cambridge, Mass:
From *Pliny's Natural History* book XX by W.H.S. Jones, translator ©1961: a quotation on leeks, reprinted by permission.

Knapp-Fishers, Solicitors, on behalf of the Trustees of Edward Verall Lucas, London:
A poem by E.V. Lucas entitled "Potatoes", reprinted by permission.

Alfred A. Knopf, Inc., New York:
From *The Physiology of Taste* by Jean Anthelme Brillat-Savarin, translated by M.F.K. Fisher ©1949: a quotation on chocolate, reprinted by permission.

New American Library, Inc., New York:
From *Chinese Meatless Cooking* by Stella Lau Fessler ©1980: a quotation by Sung Dynasty poet Su T'ung Po on soup, reprinted by permission.

Penguin Books, Ltd., London:
From *The Story of the Stone* by Cao Xuequin, translated by David Hawkes ©1973: a poem entitled "The Hopeful Sign", reprinted by permission.

A.D. Peters & Co. Ltd., Literary Agents, London:
From *A Conversation with a Cat* by Hilaire Belloc ©1931: a quotation on omelets, reprinted by permission.
From *First and Last* by Hilaire Belloc ©1911: a quotation on cheese, reprinted by permission.

Quartet Books, Ltd., a member of The Namara Group, London:
From *The Garden of Joys* by Henry Cattan ©1979: a folktale entitled "The Traveller with the Poor Appetite", reprinted by permission.

Random House, Inc., New York:
From *Alice's Restaurant Cookbook* by Alice May Brock ©1969: a quotation on international cookery, reprinted by permission.

Simon and Schuster, Inc., New York:
From *Nice Guys Finish Last* by Leo Durocher ©1975: a quotation by Babe Ruth on scallions, reprinted by permission.

The Viking Press, Inc., New York:
From *Cooking of the Maharajas* by Shivaji Rao and Shalini Devi Holkar ©1975: a folktale on the chick-pea, reprinted by permission of the author.

Vegetariana has been two very intense years in the making and during that time many people have been extraordinarily supportive, enabling me to approach this, my first book, with great pleasure and stamina. I would especially like to thank the members of my family for their enthusiasm every step of the way, as well as those friends who are too numerous to list.

For her willingness to take on a novice, and her ongoing enthusiasm, special thanks go to my editor, Frances McCullough, and also to editorial assistant Carol Chen for all her help.

Recipes and recipe ideas were contributed by Elisheva Atlas, Anne Atlas, Susan Cohen, Tzviah Iden, Angela Mascola, Ora Shapiro, Helen Tabak, Hank Virgona, and Jan Wunderman. Valuable research contributions were lent by Patrick Bunyan, and the fine mechanicals for this book were done by Sandra Fryrear of Sandra Fryrear Design.

Ron Atlas and Isaac Blech must be commended for being constant, creative sounding-boards for words and ideas. I am also grateful to Joyce Frommer and Diana Price for their involvement and interest beyond the call of duty.

These acknowledgments would be incomplete without mentioning the New York Public Library system. Were it not for the access to their incredible written and visual collections, both old and new, researching a book of this sort may have proven impossible for me.

Last, but absolutely most importantly, my utmost gratitude goes to my husband, Chaim Tabak, for being an excellent critic, for his great patience and eternal optimism, and for the countless ways in which he contributed to the making of this book.

CONTENTS

INTRODUCTION

"What on earth do you eat?" was a question I was often asked when I first became a vegetarian in the early 1970s. Even then, a meatless diet was not as widespread and accepted as it is today. I rarely hear this question any more, because so many people have cut down or eliminated meat from their diets; they have learned that the answer is, of course, a wealth of fresh vegetables and fruits, grains, legumes, tofu, nuts, seeds, dairy products, pastas, soups, salads, good breads, and yes, the occasional dessert.

Growing up with a drawing pencil in my hand, I learned early to scrutinize the things around me, and that included what was on my dinner plate. As a child, I didn't have to be urged to "finish your vegetables," but to "eat your meat." Somehow, almost by instinct, that meat or fish on my plate never appealed to any of my senses.

It was not until I was sixteen years old that I was "adult" enough to assert my way in the kitchen and declare myself a vegetarian. At first, this decision was not met with cheers from the family, but interestingly, within a few years, my parents and both of my brothers, in their separate situations and life-styles all became enthusiastic vegetarians. Having given up meat simply because I didn't like it, it was only after the fact that I became interested in exploring the health benefits and philosophies of vegetarianism, which I found fascinating. It was equally fulfilling to discover that the variety of foods I could eat broadened considerably, and that I loved to experiment with these exciting new options in cookery.

My career as an illustrator and graphic designer began almost simultaneously with my move to New York City and my marriage to a fellow artist. A veteran of artist-bachelorhood, in which eating meat and fish was more a matter of supposed convenience than desire, my husband promptly became a vegetarian when we met. Although dinners were often quick improvised concoctions made after our long days in the studio, I took pleasure in making them fun and memorable with interesting flavors, textures, colors, and aromas, using fresh, whole ingredients. My husband's enthusiasm for these unusual meals persuaded me to write down some of those recipes so that I could repeat them.

Later, as I began making dinners that pleased even nonvegetarian guests, I found myself with dozens, if not hundreds of recipes and a desire to incorporate them, somehow, with my illustrations. It was my reading *Pudd'nhead Wilson* by Mark Twain, whose witty homilies opening each chapter often referred to a food item to make a point (see pages 63 and 117) that sparked the inspiration to use literature and lore as the basis for those illustrations. The result is *Vegetariana,* a collection not merely of recipes, but also of the surprisingly literary, legendary, folkloric, poetic, and even erotic contexts in which the marvelous variety of foods in the realm of vegetarian cookery are celebrated.

In researching this book, I had at first expected to find a few quotations here and there with which to embellish the recipes. I was unprepared for the avalanche of material that kept me captivated in the library for months. It was an unexpected pleasure to find American humorists, such as Mark Twain and Josh Billings, writing on cauliflower, corn, and even cherries, and to discover that Beethoven gave serious thought to soup. It was a delight to find in Shakespeare's plays a virtual garden of herbs, and to browse through another garden—*The Perfumed Garden* —a fourteenth-century erotic manual, to unearth recipes that promised to provoke great lust.

In other realms, certain foods were honored as aids to magic, fertility, and divination, affirming the important role the edible plant kingdom has played on a multitude of levels throughout history.

Equally as fascinating and full of surprises was my exploration into the world of vegetarianism itself. Many of my generation believe that vegetarianism sprang up in the 1960s and blossomed into the new age of health consciousness of the 1970s. However, the roots of vegetarianism run as deep as ancient India, classical Greece and Rome, and the Old and New Testaments of the Bible. More recently, but perhaps even more obscure, is the story of the almost concurrent, widespread vegetarian movements in nineteenth-century America and England, attracting scores of prominent writers and reformers.

A GATHERING OF SOME EMINENT VEGETARIANS

These estimable figures are but a small sampling of well-known vegetarians of the past. Although all were staunch advocates of vegetarianism for varying reasons, some practiced this diet with greater consistency than others.

LEONARDO DA VINCI
(1452–1519)

Leonardo, despite his fascination with military machinery, was a compassionate humanitarian and a vegetarian for much of his life. His love for animals is cited as the basis for his dietary beliefs; legend has it that he bought caged birds just to set them free.

GEORGE BERNARD SHAW
(1856–1950)

"It is nearly fifty years since I was assured by a conclave of doctors that if I did not eat meat I should die of starvation."
Shaw confounded this conclave, and most likely outlived them, surviving well into his nineties as a staunch vegetarian.

LEO TOLSTOY
(1828–1910)

"And there are ideas of the future, of which some are approaching realization and are obliging people to change their way of life... such ideas in our world are those of freeing the labourers, of giving equality to women, of ceasing to use flesh food, and so on."

MOHANDAS GANDHI
(1869–1948)

This great Indian leader was a vegetarian almost all his life and gave credence to both the health benefits and ethical issues in his books and lectures. Vegetarianism, he believed, was not only a way of eating but a way of life, and contributed to one's spiritual progress.

PERCY BYSSHE SHELLEY
(1792–1822)

"There is no disease, bodily or mental, which adoption of vegetable diet and pure water has not infallibly mitigated wherever the experiment has been fairly tried."

FRANZ KAFKA
(1883–1924)

"I was sad in the evening because I had eaten anchovies. In the morning, the doctor comforted me; why be sad? After all, I ate the anchovies, not the anchovies me."

EASTERN AND WESTERN ROOTS

Vegetarianism's Far Eastern roots are well known and stem almost exclusively from the doctrine of *ahimsa,* which is common to Buddhism, Hinduism, and Jainism. *Ahimsa* is the doctrine of the sanctity of all life, of kindness, and of noninjury. It originated in Indian Vedic literature, although it was Gautama Buddha, who lived around the fifth century B.C., and the Jains who popularized the doctrine. Although kindness toward all creatures was a principle of the Buddhists, avoiding meat was not an absolute, as it was with the Jains and, for a time, among certain Hindus.

Legend has it that the Buddha's convictions on non-injury toward all creatures arose from his sorrow at seeing a family of insects destroyed by a plow.

A contemporary of the Buddha was the Greek philosopher and mathematician Pythagoras, who is perhaps better known as the originator of the Pythagorean Theorem than as the "father of Western vegetarianism." Pythagoras, like many other important Greek philosophers after him, favored a natural, meatless diet, stressing that "the earth affords a lavish supply of riches..."

Plato, who lived around the third century B.C., also advocated this diet, although there is no evidence that he himself was a vegetarian. In Plato's *Republic,* after describing the meatless bounty of which the citizens partake, he states that with such a diet they "may be expected to live in peace and health to a good old age."

THE BRITISH VEGETARIANS

The "Pythagorean Diet" is referred to by many later writers, such as Ovid, Voltaire, Emerson, and Shelley.

Percy Bysshe Shelley, the English poet, staunchly advocated vegetarianism for both health and ethical reasons, but was unable to stick to it consistently. Shelley apparently did not know how to eat well and was generally rather sickly, and so had to be constantly on the defensive about his diet:

> *The advocate of a new diet is held bound to be invulnerable by disease, in the same manner as the secretaries of a new religion are held to be more moral than other people...* (from a letter dated 1817)

Shelley wrote of the ideals of vegetarianism both in prose and poetry and it was his rather graphic poetry that influenced George Bernard Shaw, the caustic English playwright, to become a vegetarian. Shaw adhered strictly to a meatless diet for nearly seventy years, until his death at age ninety-four. Luckily for him, his wife and later his housekeeper were excellent cooks and prepared for him a wide assortment of imaginative dishes. Although he could be self-righteous on the subject of vegetarianism (he even sent his friends "vegetarian postcards" which he had printed himself), he could also be wittier than most in the same regard. An example is on page 34.

Right between Shelley and Shaw, in the mid-nineteenth century, the British Vegetarian Society was established. This movement, like its almost concurrent American counterpart, was instigated by clergymen, and stressed the health benefits of such a way of life, which also included temperance. As in the American movement, it was joined and promoted by prominent reformers, including the radical feminist Annie Besant, who embraced a form of Eastern spiritualism. For all that the two movements share in common, there seemed to have been little contact until Mrs. Besant and some Indian teachers traveled to the United States in 1893 and introduced a certain mystical element to American vegetarianism.

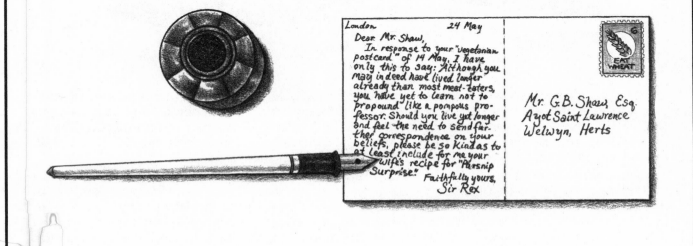

London   24 May
Dear Mr. Shaw,
    In response to your "vegetarian postcard" of 14 May, I have only this to say: Although you may indeed have lived longer already than most meat-eaters, you have yet to learn not to propound like a pompous professor. Should you live yet longer and feel the need to send further correspondence on your beliefs, please be so kind as to at least include for me your wife's recipe for "Parsnip Surprise." Faithfully yours,
                              Sir Rex

Mr. G.B. Shaw, Esq.
Ayot Saint Lawrence
Welwyn, Herts

EAT WHEAT

VEGETARIANA AMERICANA

Possibly the strongest vegetarian movement in the United States prior to the one that blossomed in the 1960s occurred around the mid-nineteenth century. Its members included many renowned reformers and literary figures. As in the British movement, the leaders were mainly clergy; perhaps the best known of those was Sylvester Graham (1794–1851), father of "Graham crackers." Originally the name was associated with Graham Bread, a coarse, whole wheat bread which he developed and promoted in his widely heard lectures, along with a natural vegetarian diet, hygiene, and temperance.

In 1850, the American Vegetarian Society was born in New York City, primarily instigated by two clergymen who had separately established "vegetarian churches." Graham was still alive to participate in the first year's meetings of the society, which was also joined by two prominent members of the Alcott family, Dr. William Alcott, and Bronson Alcott (father of Louisa May Alcott, author of *Little Women*).

These meetings, which stressed the health and longevity benefits of vegetarianism, went on well into the 1850s, hosting many notable guests at their vegetarian feasts. Among them were the feminists Amelia Bloomer, Susan B. Anthony, and Lucy Stone. The Society was very much in favor of women's rights, among other reforms.

Noted guests at Vegetarian Society feasts: Susan B. Anthony, Amelia Bloomer, Lucy Stone

Other groups were spawned, such as the Vegetarian Society of America, also a health-oriented group, whose publications in the 1880s heartily endorsed an important new diet reformer named Dr. J.H. Kellogg. Dr. Kellogg and his family were the founders of the Kellog's cereal company of Battle Creek, and it was he who originated peanut butter, corn flakes, high-protein meat substitutes, such as Protose, a certain form of granola, and other "health foods."

An assortment of vegetarian communes sprang up in the nineteenth century from various convictions and for different purposes. Perhaps the most notable yet shortest lived vegetarian community was Fruitlands, established in 1843 by Bronson Alcott and Dr. William Alcott on an 11-acre tract in Massachusetts. While William's stance against meat consumption was health-oriented, Bronson's was rigorously ethical. Apart from the Alcott family, including Louisa May (who later wrote of the Fruitlands experiment in a rather satirical piece entitled "Transcendental Wild Oats"), other members were writers and reformers of the day. Family conflicts and the members' inadequate farming abilities were among the causes that forced Fruitlands to disband after only seven months.

Henry David Thoreau (1817–1862), the author of Walden, a chronicle of simplicity in a solitary life, chose to experiment with vegetarianism in his solitude rather than as part of the general movement. Long an advocate of vegetarianism, but at best an inconsistent practitioner of it, he nevertheless wrote eloquently of vegetarian ideals:

> *One farmer says to me, "You cannot live on vegetable food solely, for it furnishes nothing to make bones with," and so he religiously devotes a part of his day to supplying his system with the raw material of bones; talking all the while he walks behind his oxen, which, with vegetable made bones, jerk him and his lumbering plow along in spite of every obstacle.* (Walden, 1854)

Turning back to the eighteenth century, we find another fascinating American who experimented with vegetarianism. Benjamin Franklin (1706–1790) gave up meat at the age of sixteen and seemed primarily to enjoy the thriftiness of such a diet. He convinced his employer, a printer who he called a "great glutton," to enter upon the experiment with him:

> *He agreed to try the practice if I would keep him company. I did so, and we held it for three months. We had our victuals dress'd, and brought to us regularly by a woman in the neighborhood, who had from me a list of forty dishes, to be prepar'd for us at different times, in all which there was neither fish, flesh, or fowl, and the whim suited me the better at this time from the cheapness of it, not costing us above eighteen pence sterling per week.* (The Autobiography of Benjamin Franklin)

The employer tired of the experiment and soon, Franklin gave in to his love of fresh fish, "returning only now and then occasionally to a vegetarian diet."

SKEWERING VEGETARIANS

During vegetarianism's heyday in England, several writers took up their pens in order to poke fun at vegetarians. In many cases, the barbs were not exactly gentle, as in G.K. Chesterton's sarcastic essays, or in some fictional pieces in which vegetarians were depicted as rather gullible or simplistic, as in the works of Charles Lamb or Thomas Holcroft. Today, when we have strength in numbers, it is easy to laugh at these less than flattering depictions.

One that I found particularly amusing was in *Erewhon,* a novel written in 1872 by Samuel Butler (1835-1902). The people of Erewhon (an anagram of "nowhere," a mock-Utopian society) give up eating meat, and after a time, one of their thinkers, the Professor, postulates that vegetables are only animals under another name, and that if meat is not allowed, it is equally sinful to eat vegetables and their seeds:

None such, he said, should be eaten, save what had died a natural death, such as fruit that was lying on the ground and about to rot, or cabbage-leaves that had turned yellow in late autumn. These and other like garbage he declared the only food that might be eaten with a clear conscience. Even so the eater must plant the pips of any apples or pears that he may have eaten, or any plum-stones, cherry stones, and the like, or he would come near to incurring the guilt of infanticide. The grain of cereals, according to him, was out of the question, for every such grain had a living soul as much as man had, and had as good a right as man to possess that soul in peace.

VEGETARIANISM IN UTOPIA

Vegetarianism in literature, when it was not being satirized, was often seen as an ideal concept and incorporated into the beliefs of Utopian societies by writers from as far back as Ovid to as recent as H. G. Wells. A charming Utopian legend was written by François Voltaire (1694–1778). A beautiful princess, Formosanta, pursues a god-like young man, Amazan, around the world, frequently guided by a magical Phoenix. She finally catches up with him on the banks of the Ganges, where the Utopia to which he belongs exists. Voltaire makes it clear that meat is not eaten in this society, whose people follow the "Pythagorean philosophy," because they revere all life. When Formosanta enters the house of Amazan and his mother, she encounters this scene:

The Phoenix, who was not without influence in the house, introduced the Princess of Babylon into a saloon, the walls of which were covered with orange-tree wood and inlaid with ivory. The inferior shepherds and shepherdesses, who were dressed in long white garments, with gold colored trimmings, served up, in a hundred plain porcelain baskets, a hundred various delicacies . . . they consisted of rice, sago, vermicelli, macaroni, omelettes, milk, eggs, cream, cheese, pastry of every kind, vegetables, fruits, particularly fragrant and grateful to the taste of which no idea can be formed in other climates; and they were accompanied with a profusion of refreshing liquors superior to the finest wine.

Voltaire's wonderful banquet of one hundred vegetarian delicacies leads perfectly back to the subject of *Vegetariana*—a celebration of the rich variety and colorful legacy of the vegetarian treats that await you in the chapters ahead.

SOUPS

**"*Of Soup and Love,
the first is best.* "**

—Thomas Fuller
Gnomologia (1732)

11

So much lore and literature exist on soup that it can only be concluded that soup touches something basic in us all.

Soup can be a clear broth full of tender-crisp vegetables, an elegant blended liquid garnished with dumplings, or a thick, stewlike combination of leftover vegetables, grains, and legumes. It can be light enough to just take the edge off the appetite, or substantial enough to be a meal. Hot, it warms you through on a chilly day; cold, it refreshes you in the summer.

The special problem of vegetarian soups is that you can't use a rich meat stock to give the soup depth of flavor. Seasonings are therefore particularly important. The amounts given here are a guideline: Taste your soups as you cook them and adjust the herbs and spices to your liking. Also, save all liquid from steaming or parboiling vegetables, and from cooking beans to use as stock in place of water. You can also make stock by boiling clean, discarded vegetable pieces, such as celery ends and leaves, carrot scrapings, potato peels, tough outer skins and leaves of onions and leeks, and then straining the liquid.

Many would agree that it was the French who made soup cookery an art form, and it was a Frenchman who had the following to say about soup:

"*It is to a dinner what a portico or a peristyle is to a building; that is to say, it is not only the first part of it, but it must be devised in such a manner as to set the tone of the banquet, in the same way as the overture of an opera announces the subject of the work.* **"**

—Grimod de la Reynière

AVOCADO GAZPACHO

The addition of avocado to this classic summer soup gives it a rich, substantial base.

For the base:
1 medium ripe avocado, peeled and quartered
²/₃ medium cucumber, peeled and coarsely chopped
³/₄ medium green pepper, coarsely chopped
2 to 3 tablespoons chopped fresh parsley
1 14-ounce (400g) can imported plum tomatoes with liquid
2 bunches scallions, chopped
3 cups tomato juice
Juice of 1 lemon
1 tablespoon minced fresh dill or 1 teaspoon dried dill
½ teaspoon dried marjoram
½ teaspoon dried basil
¼ teaspoon chili powder
Salt and freshly ground pepper to taste
1 tablespoon olive oil

For the garnish:
⅓ cucumber, finely chopped
1 small tomato, finely chopped
¼ green pepper, minced
2 tablespoons minced fresh parsley
¼ cup sliced green olives
1 small bunch scallions, finely chopped

Place the first 6 ingredients in the workbowl of a food processor or blender. Process until smooth, then transfer to a serving bowl. Stir in all the remaining base and garnish ingredients and mix thoroughly. Chill before serving. If you like, you can also garnish the soup with Garlic Croutons (page 29).

4 to 6 servings.

HOT OR COLD
TOMATO-LEEK SOUP

Since this relies on fresh, ripe tomatoes, it makes a good chilled summer soup, although it can still be made in the fall with good tomatoes and eaten hot—light but warming.

2 pounds (900g) ripe, red tomatoes
⅓ cup firmly packed fresh parsley
1 large leek
2 cloves garlic, minced
1 tablespoon olive oil
1 6-ounce (180g) can tomato paste
2 tablespoons dry red wine
1 tablespoon minced fresh dill or
**   1 teaspoon dried dill**
1½ teaspoons paprika
½ teaspoon dried marjoram
¼ teaspoon dried thyme
Salt and freshly ground pepper to taste

Cut 1½ pounds (675g) of the tomatoes into quarters and place them in the workbowl of a food processor or blender. Add the parsley and process until well puréed. Dice the remaining tomatoes and set aside.

Slice the white part of the leek into ¼-inch (⅔ cm) slices. Chop the tender, light green parts of the leaves. Reserve 2 or 3 of the tough green leaves, wash them, cut in half, and discard the rest of the green leaves. Separate the leek slices into rings by poking them through in the center. Wash carefully, removing all the grit, and put them into a large pot along with the reserved green leaves, garlic, and olive oil. Cover with 3 cups of water or vegetable stock, bring to a boil, then lower heat and simmer for 5 minutes. Add both the puréed and diced tomatoes and all the remaining ingredients and continue to simmer on low heat for 20 to 25 minutes, or until the leek rings are tender. Chill, or let stand for 30 minutes if you're serving this hot, then heat through before serving. Remove the green leaves before serving. Garnish the hot soup with Garlic Croutons (page 29), and the cold soup with a spoonful or two of yogurt in each serving.

6 servings.

"*Leeks impart brilliance to the voice.* "
—Pliny the Elder (A.D. 23–79)
Natural History

QUICK CHILLED
__ CUCUMBER SPINACH SOUP __

This is practically an instant soup, especially if you're using frozen spinach, although I recommend using fresh spinach if possible. If you're in a hurry to eat, the soup doesn't have to be chilled if your milk, yogurt, and cucumber come right out of your refrigerator.

³/₄ pound (340g) fresh spinach, stemmed, well washed, and chopped, or 1 10-ounce (285g) package frozen chopped spinach, thawed
2 cups milk
2 cups plain yogurt
1 large cucumber, grated
1 hard-boiled egg, chopped
Juice of ¹/₂ lemon
2 to 3 tablespoons minced fresh dill or 1 tablespoon dried dill
1 teaspoon good curry powder or Home-Mixed Curry (page 170)
Salt and freshly ground pepper to taste

If you're using fresh spinach, steam it until it is wilted. Transfer it to a serving bowl along with any liquid that may have formed. If you're using frozen spinach, make sure it is thoroughly thawed, and place it in your serving bowl without draining it.

Combine the milk and yogurt with the spinach. Then add the remaining ingredients and mix thoroughly. Adjust the consistency with more milk, or water as needed. Chill, if desired, or serve at once.

4 to 6 servings.

The expression "cool as a cucumber" has basis in fact—on a hot day, the inside of a cucumber stays about 20 degrees cooler than the air temperature. This cool quality is appreciated by today's cooks, but once caused great apprehension. The herbalist Nicolas Culpeper (1616–1654) said in his Herbal, *"they are under the dominion of the moon, though they are much cried out against for their coldness..."*

RUSSIAN BEET BORSCHT

Beets are not exactly a maligned vegetable, but certainly a fairly ignored one, whether in cookery, lore, or literature. They are not by any means a versatile food, but in what is perhaps their best-known domain, borscht, they are magnificent, with a color more intense than can be obtained from any other food, and so flavorful that little seasoning is needed. For those with a food processor, the preparation can be done in minutes; by hand, the grating is a bit tedious—but the results are worth it.

4 medium beets, peeled and grated
1 medium apple, peeled and grated
2 medium carrots, grated
1 medium onion, grated
Juice of 1 lemon
2 tablespoons minced fresh dill or
    2 teaspoons dried dill
Freshly ground pepper to taste
Sour cream for garnish

Place all the ingredients, except the sour cream, in a large pot with enough water to cover. Bring to a boil, cover, lower the heat, and simmer for about 40 to 45 minutes, or until all the vegetables are tender. Allow to cool, then cover and refrigerate until chilled. Top each serving with a generous scoop of sour cream.

6 to 8 servings.

"*In taking soup, it is necessary to avoid lifting too much into the spoon, or filling the mouth so full as to almost stop the breath.* **"**

—St. John the Baptist de la Salle
The Rules of Christian Manners and Civility (1695)

CHILLED POTATO SOUP

Start this refreshing yet substantial summer soup several hours before you'd like to serve it, so that the potatoes in their cooking liquid can cool down thoroughly. For a light summer supper full of fresh herbs, serve this with a good bread, followed by Tabouleh (page 44), Kuku Sabzi (page 115), and a fruity dessert.

5 or 6 medium potatoes, peeled and diced
1 small onion, minced
1 bay leaf
1 tablespoon butter
1/4 cup chopped fresh parsley
1 1/2 cups string beans, cut into 1-inch
    (2 1/2 cm) pieces and steamed
1/2 cup milk
1 cup plain yogurt or sour cream, or
    a combination
2 tablespoons minced fresh dill or
    1 tablespoon dried dill
Salt and freshly ground pepper to taste

Place the potatoes, onion, bay leaf, and butter in a large pot and add just enough water or vegetable stock to cover. Bring to a boil, then simmer, covered, over low heat until the potatoes are tender, taking care not to overcook them. Allow the potatoes to cool at room temperature, or refrigerate them overnight. When cooled, remove 1/2 cup of the diced potatoes with a slotted spoon, mash them well, and return them to the pot.

Add the remaining ingredients. Mix thoroughly and adjust the consistency with more milk, if desired. Chill before serving.

6 servings.

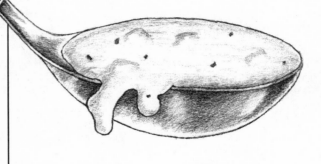

SWEET AND SOUR CABBAGE SOUP

A light soup with a subtly sweet and pungent broth, it takes the edge off the appetite without filling you up.

1/3 cup raw barley
1 large carrot, sliced
1 large celery stalk, chopped
1 medium onion, chopped
2 tablespoons butter
2 bay leaves
3 cups coarsely shredded green cabbage
1 14-ounce (400g) can imported plum
    tomatoes with liquid, chopped
3 tablespoons dry red wine
3 tablespoons red wine vinegar
2 tablespoons plus 1 teaspoon brown
    sugar
2 teaspoons paprika
1/2 teaspoon dried thyme
Salt and freshly ground pepper to taste

Place the barley, carrot, celery, onion, butter, and bay leaves in a large pot and cover with 4 1/2 cups of water or vegetable stock. Bring to a boil, then add all the remaining ingredients. Cover and simmer over low heat for 30 to 35 minutes, or until the vegetables and barley are tender, but not overcooked. Allow the soup to stand for an hour before serving, then heat through. This is also a good soup to make a day ahead.

6 to 8 servings.

In times past, a child's inquiry as to where babies come from was met with a variety of quaint responses. Do you remember being told that the stork brought you, or that you came from the cabbage patch?

MUSHROOM BARLEY SOUP

I couldn't resist including my version of this warming, comforting classic soup that is so good in the winter.

3/4 cup raw barley
1 large onion, chopped
1 large carrot, sliced
2 bay leaves
2 tablespoons butter
1 medium potato, peeled and cut into
  small dice
1 large celery stalk, finely chopped
1/4 cup chopped fresh parsley
1 tablespoon minced fresh dill, or 1
  teaspoon dried dill
1/2 teaspoon dried summer savory
Salt and freshly ground pepper to taste
1/2 pound (225g) mushrooms, coarsely
  chopped
2 cups milk
2 tablespoons unbleached white flour

Place the barley, onion, carrot, bay leaves, and butter in a large pot with 2 1/2 cups of water or vegetable stock. Bring to a boil, cover, and simmer over low heat for 10 minutes.

Add the potato, celery, parsley, and seasonings. Cover and simmer for 15 minutes. Add the mushrooms and milk, cover, and simmer over very low heat for about 20 minutes, or until the vegetables are tender but not overdone.

Dissolve the flour in just enough water to make a smooth, flowing paste and whisk it quickly into the soup. Allow the soup to stand for 5 to 10 minutes off the heat before serving. The soup thickens quite a bit if it is refrigerated. Add more milk or vegetable stock, as needed, and adjust the seasonings.

6 to 8 servings.

In parts of Southeast Asia, it was believed that coming across mushrooms at the outset of a journey foretold good fortune.

MEDITERRANEAN BROCCOLI AND MUSHROOM SOUP

This is one of those soups that develops more and more flavor as it stands. It's a good soup to make a day ahead, and it keeps very well up to four days.

1 medium onion, chopped
1/3 cup raw barley or 1/3 cup raw orzo
    (rice-shaped pasta)
2 bay leaves
2 cloves garlic, minced
1 tablespoon olive oil
2 1/2 to 3 cups finely chopped broccoli
1/2 pound (225g) coarsely chopped
    mushrooms
1 small turnip, peeled and diced
1 8-ounce (225g) can imported plum
    tomatoes with liquid, chopped
3 tablespoons minced fresh parsley
1/4 cup dry red wine
1 teaspoon paprika
1 teaspoon dried marjoram
1/2 teaspoon dried oregano
1/2 teaspoon dried basil
1/4 teaspoon dried rosemary
Salt and freshly ground pepper to taste
Grated Parmesan cheese for topping,
    optional

Place the onion, barley, bay leaves, garlic, and oil in a large pot and cover with 2 cups of water or vegetable stock. Bring to a boil, cover, and simmer over low heat for 10 minutes. (If you use the orzo instead of the barley, cook it separately until it is *al dente*, drain, and set it aside. Add it to the soup just before serving.)

Add all the remaining ingredients to the pot along with an additional 2 1/2 cups of water or stock. Cover and simmer over low heat for about 35 minutes, or until the vegetables and barley are tender. Ideally, this soup should stand at least an hour before serving. Sprinkle each serving with grated Parmesan cheese, if desired.

6 to 8 servings.

CURRIED SPINACH AND CHICK-PEA SOUP

This mildly curried soup is an inviting mixture of interesting flavors, textures, and colors.

2 tablespoons butter
2 cloves garlic, minced or crushed
1 medium carrot, coarsely grated
1/4 cup raw barley
1 bay leaf
4 cups cooked or canned chick-peas
    (about 1 2/3 cups raw, cooked following
    the directions on page 179)
3/4 pound (340g) spinach, stemmed, well
    washed, steamed and chopped or 1
    10-ounce (285g) package frozen
    chopped spinach, thawed
1 small zucchini, diced
1 1/2 teaspoons good curry powder or
    Home-Mixed Curry (page 170), or more
    to taste
1/4 teaspoon dried thyme
1/4 teaspoon ground cumin
Salt and freshly ground pepper to taste
2 cups milk
2 tablespoons lemon juice

Heat the butter in a large pot until it foams. Add the garlic and sauté for 1 minute. Add 2 1/2 cups water or vegetable stock along with the carrot, barley, and bay leaf. Bring to a boil, cover, and simmer over low heat for 15 minutes.

Mash or purée half of the chick-peas. Add them to the pot along with the spinach, zucchini, and seasonings, and simmer, covered, for 10 minutes longer.

Add the remaining chick-peas, the milk, and lemon juice. Simmer over very low heat for 15 minutes longer, or until the barley is tender.

8 or more servings.

SOUP

I saw a famous man eating soup.
I say he was lifting a fat broth
Into his mouth with a spoon.
His name was in the newspapers
*   that day*
Spelled out in tall black headlines
And thousands of people were
*   talking about him.*

When I saw him,
He sat bending his head over a plate
Putting soup in his mouth with
*   a spoon.*

—Carl Sandburg
Smoke and Steel (1920)

___ POTATO-CORN CHOWDER ___

1 medium onion, chopped
3 medium potatoes, scrubbed well and
**   diced (don't peel)**
2 medium carrots, sliced
1 large celery stalk, chopped
2 bay leaves
2 tablespoons butter
3 cups cooked fresh or (thawed) frozen
**   corn kernels**
1 14-ounce (400g) can imported plum
**   tomatoes with liquid, chopped**
1½ teaspoons ground coriander
1 teaspoon dried summer savory
½ teaspoon dried thyme
Salt and freshly ground pepper to taste
1 cup milk

Place the onion, potatoes, carrots, celery, bay leaves, and butter in a large pot with just enough water or vegetable stock to cover. Bring to a boil, cover, and simmer over low heat for 10 minutes.

Add the corn kernels, the tomatoes with their liquid, and the seasonings, and simmer, covered, over low heat, for about 20 minutes, or until all the vegetables are done to taste. Use a slotted spoon to remove ¾ cup of the potatoes. Mash them well and return them to the pot. Add the milk and stir well. Cover and simmer for 5 minutes longer.

8 servings.

JOHN DOUGH
EMBEZZLES
$1.2 MILLION
FROM ORPHANAGES

BAROMETER SOUP

I knew, by my scientific reading, that either thermometers or barometers ought to be boiled to make them accurate; I did not know which it was, so I boiled both. There was still no result...I hunted up another barometer; it was new and perfect. I boiled it half an hour in a pot of bean soup which the cooks were making. The result was unexpected: the instrument was not affected at all, but there was such a strong barometer taste to the soup that the head cook, who was a most conscientious person, changed its name in the bill of fare. The dish was so greatly liked by all, that I ordered the cook to have barometer soup every day.

—Mark Twain
  A Tramp Abroad (1880)

HEARTY BEAN SOUP

Even without a barometer, I think the filling and flavorful bean soups on this page would have pleased Mark Twain. They are good to make a day ahead; they keep well for the better part of a week and develop flavor as they stand. Although there is the option of using canned beans, it is really preferable to use raw beans for these.

2 cups cooked or canned great northern beans (about ¾ cup raw)
2 cups cooked or canned kidney or red beans (about ¾ cup raw)
2 tablespoons olive oil
1 medium onion, chopped
2 large celery stalks, chopped
1 medium potato, scrubbed and diced (don't peel)
¾ cup string beans, cut into 1-inch (2½ cm) pieces, optional
1 14-ounce (400g) can imported plum tomatoes with liquid, chopped
¼ cup dry red wine
1 teaspoon dried summer savory
1 teaspoon paprika
½ teaspoon ground coriander
½ teaspoon ground cumin
Salt and freshly ground pepper to taste

Cook the beans following the directions on page 179. Use extra water in cooking them so it can be used as stock.

Place the olive oil, onion, celery, potato, and string beans in a large pot with just enough water or vegetable stock, including the beans' cooking liquid, to cover. Bring to a boil, cover, and simmer until the vegetables are just tender. Add the beans and all the remaining ingredients plus 2 more cups of water or vegetable stock. Simmer, covered, over low heat for 20-25 minutes. Taste to be sure that everything is done to your liking.

8 or more servings.

WHITE BEAN AND ZUCCHINI SOUP

2½ cups cooked or canned white beans such as navy, small white, or great northern beans (about 1 cup raw)
1 large onion, chopped
¼ cup raw barley
2 tablespoons butter
2 bay leaves
1 heaping cup shredded white cabbage
2 medium zucchini, diced
1 small turnip, peeled and diced
1 teaspoon ground cumin
1 teaspoon dried summer savory
½ teaspoon dry mustard
½ teaspoon ground coriander
Salt and freshly ground pepper to taste
1 cup milk

Cook the beans following the directions on page 179. Do not drain any of their cooking stock.

Place the onion, barley, butter, and bay leaves in a large pot and cover with 4 cups of water or vegetable stock, including the stock from cooking the beans. Bring to a boil, cover, and simmer over low heat for 10 minutes. Add the cabbage and simmer for 10 minutes longer. Add the beans and remaining ingredients and simmer, covered, over very low heat for about 20 minutes, or until the vegetables and barley are tender. Adjust the consistency with more vegetable stock as needed. This is good with a spoonful or two of plain yogurt stirred into each serving.

8 servings.

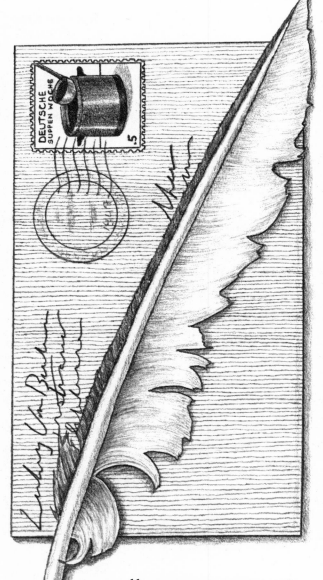

> **" Whoever tells a lie cannot be pure in heart—and only the pure in heart can make a good soup. "**
>
> —Ludwig van Beethoven
> in a letter to
> Mme. Streicher (1817)

CHEDDAR CHEESE-GARLIC SOUP

Melting the cheese down before adding the smoothly puréed vegetables assures a wonderfully velvety texture. This elegant soup is one of my special occasion favorites.

3 tablespoons butter
8 cloves garlic, crushed or minced
1 small onion, chopped
2 medium celery stalks, finely chopped
1 14-ounce (400g) can imported plum tomatoes with liquid, chopped
3 tablespoons unbleached white flour
1 pound (450g) mild Cheddar cheese, grated or cut into small dice
3 tablespoons dry white wine
1½ cups milk
1 teaspoon paprika
½ teaspoon dry mustard
Salt and freshly ground pepper to taste

Heat half the butter in a large heavy soup pot until it foams. Add the garlic, onion, and celery and sauté over very low heat, stirring frequently, until the onion is translucent. Cover with 1 cup of water and simmer, covered, over low heat until the onion and celery are quite tender. Transfer to the workbowl of a food processor or blender along with the cooking liquid and process until thoroughly puréed. Add the tomatoes and purée again until smooth.

In the same soup pot, heat the remaining butter until it foams. Add the flour, and stir with a wooden spoon until it is completely blended with the butter. Add the cheese and stir constantly over very low heat, until melted to a velvety texture. If the cheese seems to stick to the pot, add tiny amounts of water.

Slowly stir in the puréed mixture until everything is thoroughly blended. Add the remaining ingredients and simmer, uncovered, over low heat just until heated through, stirring frequently. Serve with any of the Soup Extras (page 29), or garnish with a few freshly steamed broccoli florets.

6 servings.

DILLED POTATO AND DUTCH CHEESE SOUP

As warming and soothing as this soup is when served hot, it is also excellent chilled.

6 medium potatoes, peeled and diced
1 large onion, chopped
2 cloves garlic, minced
2 bay leaves
2 tablespoons butter
1 cup milk
1 1/2 cups grated Edam or Gouda cheese
2 tablespoons unbleached white flour
2 tablespoons dry white wine
3 tablespoons minced fresh dill or 1 to 1 1/2 tablespoons dried dill
1 teaspoon paprika
1/2 teaspoon dry mustard
Salt and freshly ground pepper to taste

Place the potatoes, onion, garlic, bay leaves, and butter in a large pot and add just enough water or vegetable stock to cover. Bring to a boil, cover, lower the heat, and simmer until the potatoes are done but still firm.

Use a slotted spoon to remove 2/3 cup of the potatoes. Mash them well and return them to the pot. Add the milk, and then stir in the cheese, a little at a time. Dissolve the flour in just enough water to make a smooth, flowing paste and whisk it into the soup.

Add the remaining ingredients, cover, and simmer over very low heat for 10 to 15 minutes. Remove from the heat and let stand about 30 minutes before serving. Adjust the consistency by adding more milk as needed, then heat through.

6 or more servings.

"*I had rather live with Cheese and Garlicke in a windmill. *"

—William Shakespeare
1st *Henry IV,* (ca. 1597)

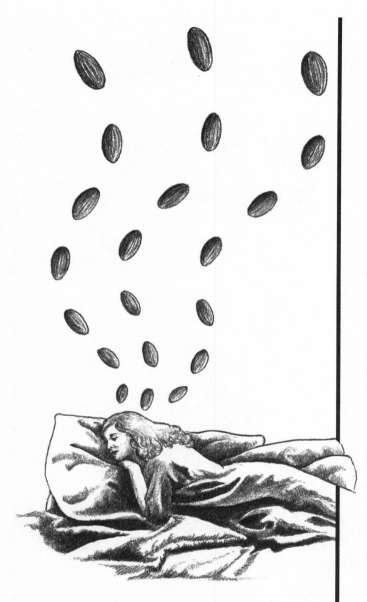

Should you dream of almonds, according to folk-belief, it means that you will embark on a journey. If the dream-almonds taste sweet, the journey will be a prosperous one.

ALMOND CREAM OF BROCCOLI SOUP

I've always found broccoli to be highly compatible with almonds. They and the apple add a nice sweet touch to this soup.

1½ pounds (675g) broccoli
1 medium onion, chopped
1 large celery stalk, chopped
1 medium tart apple, peeled, cored, and diced
2 tablespoons butter
½ cup almonds
1 tablespoon minced fresh dill or 1 teaspoon dried dill
½ teaspoon dried basil
¼ teaspoon dried thyme
Salt and freshly ground pepper to taste
3 tablespoons unbleached white flour
Juice of ½ lemon
1 cup milk
Chopped almonds for garnish

Remove and discard the tough ends of the broccoli stems (about 1½ to 2 inches, 4 to 5 cm), and chop the remaining broccoli into 1- to 2-inch (2½ to 5 cm) pieces. Place them in a large pot along with the onion, celery, apple and butter, and just enough water or vegetable stock to cover. Bring to a boil, cover, and simmer over low heat for 5 minutes. Use a slotted spoon to remove about ¾ cup of the smaller florets and set them aside for garnish. Cover and continue to simmer until the vegetables are quite tender, then remove the pot from the heat.

Place the almonds in the workbowl of a food processor or blender and process until they are as finely ground as possible. Transfer the cooked vegetables to the processor or blender with a slotted spoon, half at a time if necessary, and process them until they are well puréed. Stir the purée back into the liquid in the soup pot. Return to low heat and stir in the seasonings.

Dissolve the flour in just enough water to form a smooth, flowing paste, and whisk it into the soup. Add the lemon juice, milk, and reserved broccoli pieces and simmer just until heated through. Adjust the consistency with more vegetable stock or milk. Garnish each serving with a small amount of chopped almonds.

6 servings.

CREAM OF ASPARAGUS AND STRING BEAN SOUP

This smooth, green purée really is a Beautiful Soup.

1 pound (450g) asparagus, cut into 1-inch (2½ cm) pieces
1 pound (450g) string beans, cut into 1-inch (2½ cm) pieces
1 medium onion, chopped
2 cloves garlic, minced
1 medium potato, scrubbed and diced (don't peel)
2 tablespoons butter
2 bay leaves
2 tablespoons unbleached white flour
1 teaspoon dried basil
¾ teaspoon dried dill
Salt and freshly ground pepper to taste
½ to 1 cup milk

Cut off the tips of the asparagus and reserve them; while soup is cooking, steam them until they are tender-crisp.

Combine the first 7 ingredients in a large pot with barely enough water or vegetable stock to cover. Bring to a boil, then cover and simmer on low heat until the vegetables are quite tender.

Transfer the vegetables to the workbowl of a food processor or blender, half at a time, and process until very smoothly puréed. Return to the pot and stir into the reserved liquid, and return to low heat.

Dissolve the flour in just enough water to form a smooth, flowing paste and whisk it into the soup. Add the seasonings and simmer for 2 to 3 minutes. Add enough milk to achieve desired consistency, followed by the steamed asparagus tips, and simmer just until heated through.

This soup thickens as it is refrigerated—add small amounts of milk or vegetable stock to thin, and adjust seasonings. Serve garnished with any of the Soup Extras (page 29).

6 servings.

Beautiful Soup, so rich and green,
Waiting in a hot tureen!
Who for such dainties would not stoop?
Soup of the evening, beautiful Soup!
Soup of the evening, beautiful Soup!
*   Beau—ootiful Soo—oop!*
*   Beau—ootiful Soo—oop!*
Soo—oop of the e—e—vening,
*   Beautiful, beautiful Soup!*

Beautiful Soup! Who cares for fish,
Game, or any other dish?
Who would not give all else for two
Pennyworth only of beautiful Soup?
Pennyworth only of beautiful Soup?
*   Beau—ootiful Soo—oop!*
*   Beau—ootiful Soo—oop!*
Soo—oop of the e—e—vening,
*   Beau—ootiful, beautiFUL SOUP!*

—Lewis Carroll
Alice's Adventures in Wonderland (1865)

THE TRAVELLER WITH THE POOR APPETITE

A traveller came upon a hermit who lived alone in a mountain cave near Jericho and asked him if he had anything to give him to eat. The hermit invited his visitor to sit down, and brought a loaf of bread which he placed in front of him. He then went again to fetch him a plate of lentil soup. On his return he was amazed to find that his visitor had already eaten the loaf of bread. So he placed the plate of soup in front of him and went again to fetch some more bread. Returning with another loaf, he discovered that the visitor had already devoured the soup. This business went on for awhile, the hermit rushing to and fro, no sooner bringing the bread than the soup had gone, and no sooner getting more soup than the bread was eaten up.

The hermit paused and asked the visitor the object of his journey. The visitor explained that he was on his way to a famous doctor in Damascus whose treatment he sought because his appetite was poor. On his way back, he added, he would stop and pay him his respects. Alarmed by the traveller's future plans, especially should the famous doctor of Damascus succeed in improving his appetite even further, the hermit told his visitor not to try to see him on his way back, as on the morrow he would be leaving on a pilgrimage and would be away for a long, long time. "In any case," he added, "I bid you good-bye in advance!"

—Arabic folk-tale
  retold by Henry Cattan in
  The Garden of Joys (1979)

LENTIL AND BROWN RICE SOUP

With its complementary proteins of lentils and rice, and its savory flavors, this is one of the "everyday" soups I like best. A good choice when you want to serve soup as the main course; a good bread, a hearty salad such as Colorful Cabbage Salad (page 34) and a fruity dessert would round this meal out nicely.

1/2 **cup raw lentils, picked over and washed**
1/3 **cup raw brown rice**
2 **tablespoons olive oil**
2 **cloves garlic, minced**
2 **tablespoons soy sauce**
2 **bay leaves**
1 **small onion, finely chopped**
2 **medium carrots, thinly sliced**
1 **large celery stalk, finely chopped**
Handful of chopped celery leaves
1 **14-ounce (400g) can imported plum**
   tomatoes with liquid, chopped
1/2 **cup tomato sauce or tomato juice**
1/4 **cup dry red wine or dry sherry**
1 **teaspoon dried basil**
1 **teaspoon paprika**
1/2 **teaspoon dried marjoram**
1/2 **teaspoon dried thyme**
Salt and freshly ground pepper to taste

Place the first 6 ingredients in a large pot and cover with 3 cups of water. Bring to a boil, cover and simmer over low heat for 7 to 8 minutes.

Add 2 additional cups of water along with all the remaining ingredients. Cover and simmer over low heat for 25 to 30 minutes, or until the vegetables, rice, and lentils are done to your liking.

6 servings.

CREAM OF CELERY AND CORN SOUP

No baskets here, Mr. Hubbard.

8 large celery stalks
Handful of chopped celery leaves
1 medium onion, chopped
2 medium potatoes, peeled and diced
2½ cups cooked fresh or (thawed) frozen corn kernels
1 teaspoon dried dill
½ teaspoon dried thyme
¼ teaspoon ground coriander
Salt and freshly ground pepper to taste
1 to 1½ cups milk, or as necessary
2 tablespoons butter

Cut 6 of the celery stalks into 1-inch (2½ cm) pieces. Place them in a large pot along with the leaves, the onion, and potatoes. Add just enough water to cover. Bring to a boil, cover, lower the heat, and simmer until the vegetables are quite tender. Remove from the heat.

Use a slotted spoon to transfer the vegetables to the workbowl of a food processor or blender. Process until the mixture is fairly smooth, then add 2 cups of the corn kernels and process until well puréed. (You may have to do this half at a time.) Return to the soup pot and stir the purée into the reserved liquid. Return to moderately low heat. Add the seasonings, milk, and remaining corn, and allow to simmer, uncovered.

Chop the 2 remaining celery stalks into small dice. Heat the butter in a small skillet. When the butter foams, add the celery and sauté over low heat until lightly browned. Stir the celery into the soup and simmer just until the soup is thoroughly heated through. Garnish with Garlic Croutons (page 29).

6 servings.

Nowadays, we don't eat very much pumpkin except in pie, but it was a staple food for the Pilgrims of Plymouth Colony. They were so innundated with it that they invented this little song:

We have pumpkin at morning
And pumpkin at noon
If it were not for pumpkin
We would be undoon.

PUMPKIN SOUP

Once you have your cooked beans ready, this slightly eccentric soup can be made in about half an hour.

**2 cups cooked or canned navy or small
    white beans (about ¾ cup raw)**
**1 medium zucchini, quartered lengthwise
    and sliced**
1½ cups coarsely chopped mushrooms
2 tablespoons butter
2 bay leaves
**2 cups cooked, puréed pumpkin or
    1 16-ounce (450g) can plain,
    unsweetened pumpkin**
½ cup sliced black olives
½ teaspoon nutmeg
½ teaspoon dried sage
½ teaspoon ground coriander
Salt and freshly ground pepper to taste

Cook the beans following the directions on page 179. Cook them in extra water so you can use it as stock.

Place the zucchini, mushrooms, butter, and bay leaves in a large pot with 3 cups of water or vegetable stock, including the beans' cooking liquid. Bring to a boil, lower the heat, and add all the remaining ingredients. Cover and simmer just until the zucchini and mushrooms are tender, about 10 minutes. Adjust the consistency with more vegetable stock or water as needed.

6 servings.

CHINESE VEGETABLE MISO SOUP

Miso is a concentrated, high-protein paste made from soybeans whose salty flavor is reminiscent of soy sauce. Look for it in health food stores or in Oriental groceries. This soup is best when eaten immediately; don't plan on having more than one day's worth of leftover soup.

1 tablespoon sesame oil
2 celery stalks, sliced diagonally
1 medium carrot, sliced thin
2 cloves garlic, minced
1 heaping cup raw vermicelli, buckwheat noodles, or other thin Chinese noodles, broken into 2-inch (5 cm) pieces
1 medium turnip, peeled and diced
2 to 3 bunches scallions, chopped (white and green parts kept separate)
1½ cups chopped mushrooms
¾ cup snow peas, cut into 1-inch (2½ cm) pieces
1 cup firmly packed fresh mung bean sprouts
2 tablespoons dry sherry
1 tablespoon white or rice vinegar
2 cakes tofu (bean curd), diced
4 tablespoons miso, or to taste

Bring 5 cups of water or vegetable stock to a boil in a large pot. Lower the heat and add the sesame oil, celery, carrot, and garlic. Cover and simmer over low heat for 10 minutes.

In the meantime, cook the noodles separately. When they are cooked *al dente*, drain them and set them aside.

Add the turnip and the white parts of the scallions to the pot, cover, and simmer for 5 minutes. Then add the remaining ingredients, except the tofu, miso, and noodles, and simmer, covered, until all the vegetables are cooked to a tender-crisp texture. Add the noodles and tofu and remove from heat.

Dissolve the miso thoroughly in ½ cup warm water. Stir into the soup. If you've never had miso before, try pouring half in and tasting it before you pour the rest.

6 servings.

SOUP EXTRAS

COTTAGE CHEESE MATZO DUMPLINGS

Dumplings can sometimes be a great fuss to make, but these, a variation on matzo balls, are quite simple and really give substance to a puréed soup.

2 eggs, well beaten
⅓ cup small curd cottage cheese
1 tablespoon vegetable or safflower oil
1 cup matzo meal
½ teaspoon salt

Combine the beaten eggs with the cottage cheese and oil. Stir in the matzo meal and salt and mix thoroughly. Cover and refrigerate for 1 hour. This will make the batter very easy to handle.

Bring a large pot of water to a boil. In the meantime, shape the batter into ¾- to 1-inch (2 to 2½ cm) balls. When the water reaches a rolling boil, drop the balls in and allow to cook at a slow boil for 12 minutes. Remove with a skimmer and drain before using.

This makes about 18 dumplings.

GARLIC CROUTONS

Simply take as many slices of whole grain bread as needed, preferably several days old, and rub them with the inside of a clove of garlic. Cut the bread into small cubes and arrange on a baking sheet. Bake at 300°F (150°C), stirring occasionally, until brown and crisp.

WHEAT BERRIES

The nutty taste and chewy texture of whole wheat berries make for an interestingly different soup garnish. Cook following the directions on page 178. If you'd like, you can sauté them in a little butter and soy sauce or tamari before adding them to the soup.

"When hungry, vegetable soup, beans, and corn can equal the taste of rare dainties. "

—Su Tung-p'o,
Sung Dynasty Poet

SALADS

"*According to a Spanish proverb, four persons are wanted to make a salad: a spendthrift for oil, a miser for vinegar, a counsellor for salt, and a madman to stir it all up.*"

—Abraham Hayward
The Art of Dining (1854)

Preparations of fresh, raw or semi-cooked vegetables mixed with herbs and spices, dressed in oils, vinegars, and juices have been made since time immemorial. Salad-making has been recorded in the Bible and in various writings of ancient Greece and Rome and medieval Europe among others. In some ways, the salad of yesteryear may have been more sophisticated than today's, due to the greater awareness of usable herbs, and even flowers.

Rather than going into ways of combining seasonal greens, which most salad-lovers do as a matter of course, this chapter takes a more offbeat approach to the salad. Some, which utilize grains, beans, and cheeses, are hearty enough to constitute the main dish of a summer meal. Others present vegetables better known for their use in hot dishes with an unusual twist.

"In the composure of a sallet every plant should come in to bear its part, without being overpower'd by some herb of a stronger taste, so as to endanger the native sapor and virtue of the rest, but fall into their places, like the notes in music, in which there should be nothing harsh or grating: and tho' admitting some discords (to distinguish and illustrate the rest), striking in the more sprightly, and sometimes gentler notes, reconcile all dissonance and melt them into an agreeable composition. "

—John Evelyn
   *Acetaria: A Discourse
   of Sallet* (1699)

LENTIL AND FETA CHEESE SALAD

A substantial, high-protein salad with a Greek flavor, this is a good choice when you want salad to be the main part of your meal, whether for lunch or supper.

1 cup raw lentils, sorted, washed, and cooked following the directions on page 179
1 medium green pepper, chopped
2 medium firm, ripe tomatoes, chopped
1 small red or white onion, chopped, optional
1/2 pound (225g) feta cheese, crumbled
1/4 cup olive oil
Juice of 1 lemon
2 tablespoons red wine vinegar
1 teaspoon dried basil
1 teaspoon dried dill
1 teaspoon dried summer savory
Salt and freshly ground pepper to taste
Dark green lettuce of your choice

For garnish:
Greek black olives
Hard-boiled eggs
Lemon wedges

Allow the cooked lentils to cool to room temperature.

Transfer the lentils to a mixing bowl and combine with the remaining ingredients, except the lettuce and garnishes. Although this salad may be served immediately, ideally it should be allowed to stand, refrigerated, 1 to 2 hours.

Prepare a bed of lettuce for each serving, and garnish with the olives, hard-boiled eggs, and lemon wedges.

6 to 8 servings.

MARINATED BROCCOLI AND CAULIFLOWER

I have found this salad to be a favorite at parties; it looks as appealing as it tastes, especially if you are able to use red peppers. You'll find that it complements almost any of the Italian-style pasta recipes very nicely.

4 heaping cups cauliflower, cut into bite-size pieces and florets
4 heaping cups broccoli, cut as above
1 medium sweet red or green pepper, cut into julienne strips
1 small onion, cut in half and sliced
2/3 cup Herb Marinade (page 55)
2 tablespoons lemon juice
Salt and freshly ground pepper to taste
1/2 teaspoon dill seed, optional
1/2 teaspoon dried tarragon, optional

Fill a large pot with water and bring to a full, rolling boil. You will need enough water to immerse all the cauliflower and broccoli. Drop the cauliflower and broccoli pieces into the boiling water, and cook over high heat for no longer than 3 minutes, or to a tender-crisp texture. Drain (reserve the liquid to use as vegetable stock for soup) and splash with cool water until the vegetables stop steaming.

Place the red pepper and onion in a large mixing bowl. Add the cauliflower and broccoli to the mixing bowl. Pour the marinade over the vegetables and then add the remaining ingredients. Toss to mix well and refrigerate for several hours, stirring occasionally to distribute the marinade.

6 to 8 servings.

"*A wise man is the proper composer of an excellent sallet, and how many transcendancies belong to an accomplish'd sallet-dresser, so as to emerge an exact critic indeed.*"

—John Evelyn
Acetaria: A Discourse of Sallet (1699)

O Sallet! With how many exactitudes have I dressed thee?

COLORFUL CABBAGE SALAD

If cabbages really did have feelings, they'd be somewhat hurt, because they are a vegetable fairly frequently maligned in literature. This was not so in classical Greece and Rome, where cabbage was highly praised by Pliny and others for its nutritive qualities and was also believed to have the ability to prevent drunkenness. Cabbage gives salads such crispness and substance that I'm devoting these two pages to it—so start crunching.

2½ cups thinly shredded cabbage
1 cup halved cherry tomatoes
1 large carrot, coarsely grated
⅓ cup chopped or sliced black olives
¾ cup diced mozzarella cheese, optional
2 bunches scallions, finely chopped
2 tablespoons finely chopped
**   fresh parsley**
Salt and freshly ground pepper to taste
Yogurt-Dill Dressing (page 56)

Combine all the ingredients in a serving bowl. Pass the Yogurt-Dill Dressing around with the salad.

4 to 6 servings.

"*When I tell people that I am a vegetarian, I am always told that cabbages also have feelings.* **"**

—George Bernard Shaw

CABBAGE-APPLE COOLER

Cabbage and apples in yogurt combine to make a very good palate-cooling salad to be served with spicy dishes.

2½ cups thinly shredded red or white
**   cabbage**
1 medium apple, peeled and diced
¼ cup raisins
1 small carrot, coarsely grated
1 tablespoon sesame or poppy seeds
1 to 2 tablespoons minced fresh mint
**   leaves, or 1 to 2 teaspoons dried mint**
1 cup plain yogurt
Juice of ½ lemon
1 teaspoon sesame oil
2 tablespoons honey

Combine the first 6 ingredients in a large bowl.

Combine the yogurt, lemon juice, sesame oil, and honey in a small bowl. Mix thoroughly, and pour over the cabbage mixture. Toss until thoroughly combined. Chill before serving.

6 servings.

SUNFLOWER COLESLAW

Sunflower seeds add a nice, nutty flavor to this coleslaw.

**3 cups thinly shredded white or
    red cabbage**
2 medium carrots, coarsely grated
Juice of 1 lemon
**3 tablespoons finely chopped fresh
    parsley**
¼ cup toasted sunflower seeds
Freshly ground pepper to taste
**1 cup of Tofu "Mayonnaise" (page 52) or
    1 cup Parsley Dressing (page 57)**

Combine all the ingredients in a bowl and mix thoroughly. If you're using the Parsley Dressing, eliminate the 3 tablespoons fresh parsley. Chill before serving.

6 to 8 servings.

" *The Floure of the Sunne is called in Latin Flos Solis; for that some have reported it to turn with the Sunne...but I rather think it was so called because it resembles the radiant beams of the Sunne...* **"**

—John Gerarde
  The Herball (1636)

HEARTY PASTA AND RED BEAN SALAD

Pasta salads are a satisfying yet surprisingly light lunch or supper dish in the summer, although there is no reason not to have them year round.

2 cups raw, medium-sized shaped pasta, such as rotelle, ziti, etc.
2 cups cooked or canned red or kidney beans (about ¾ cup raw, cooked following the directions on page 179)
1 cup diced zucchini (approximately 1 medium zucchini)
1 small green pepper, finely chopped
1 medium-sized ripe tomato, chopped
⅓ cup chopped green olives
¼ cup grated Parmesan cheese
1 cup plain yogurt, or 1 cup Tofu "Mayonnaise" (page 52)
½ teaspoon chili powder, or more to taste
½ teaspoon ground coriander
½ teaspoon paprika
¼ teaspoon dried sage
Salt and freshly ground pepper to taste

Cook the pasta *al dente* and rinse with cool water. Drain the pasta well and put it in a mixing bowl. Add the remaining ingredients and mix thoroughly. Serve at room temperature or chilled.

6 servings.

> **"You can put everything, and the more things the better, into salad, as into a conversation; but everything depends upon the skill of mixing."**
> —Charles Dudley Warner
> *My Summer in a Garden* (1871)

PASTA SALAD WITH ARTICHOKES AND SPROUTS

The artichoke hearts provide an instant marinade, and the alfalfa sprouts lend an interesting texture.

2 cups raw small, shaped pasta, such as small shells or elbows, etc.
¾ pound (340 g) marinated artichoke hearts, either 2 6-ounce (180g) jars, or bought by weight
¾ cup firmly packed alfalfa sprouts
1 small green pepper, finely chopped
1 medium carrot, coarsely grated
½ cup sliced or chopped black olives
¼ cup red wine vinegar, more or less to taste
½ teaspoon dried basil
½ teaspoon dried summer savory
Salt and freshly ground pepper to taste

Cook the pasta *al dente*, then rinse it with cool water. Drain the pasta well and put it in a mixing bowl.

Chop the artichokes into bite-sized pieces and add them to the pasta. Add the alfalfa sprouts, separating the strands as much as possible with a fork, and the remaining ingredients. Mix well and allow to stand for 1 to 2 hours either at room temperature or refrigerated before serving.

4 to 6 servings.

Variation: To serve as a main dish salad, garnish with hard-boiled eggs or add some diced mozzarella cheese.

> **"To make a good salad is to be a brilliant diplomat: one must know exactly how much oil one must put with one's vinegar."**
> —Oscar Wilde (1856–1900)

'Twas a good lady; we may pick a thousand salads, ere we light on such another herb.

Indeed, sir, she was the sweet marjoram of the salad, or rather the herb of grace.

—William Shakespeare
All's Well That Ends Well (ca. 1602)

MARINATED SPROUTS AND STRING BEANS

If you like fresh bean sprouts, this is an attractive way to serve them in a salad. Beware of tough-skinned string beans; choose the smaller, more tender ones.

3 heaping cups string beans, cut into 1-inch (2½ cm) pieces
2½ cups (about ½ pound, 225g) fresh mung bean sprouts
1 medium carrot, coarsely grated
2 tablespoons finely minced onion
½ cup Herb Marinade (page 55)
Salt and freshly ground pepper to taste

Steam the string beans and bean sprouts separately to a tender-crisp texture. Combine in a mixing bowl and allow them to cool until they stop steaming. (This would be a good time to make the marinade if you don't have any on hand.)

Add the remaining ingredients to the bowl and mix thoroughly. Marinate for several hours, refrigerated, stirring occasionally to distribute the marinade.

Serve on a bed of dark green lettuce leaves.

4 to 6 servings.

CUCUMBER RAITA

A raita is a traditional Indian salad with yogurt served for the purpose of cooling the palate alongside a hot curry dish. Cucumber is excellent for this purpose, since it has cooling properties of its own.

1 large cucumber, chopped
1 cup plain yogurt
1 teaspoon safflower or vegetable oil
¼ cup chopped cilantro or fresh parsley
1 teaspoon dry mint, or
     1 tablespoon minced fresh mint, or
     more to taste
Pinch of ground cumin
Salt and freshly ground pepper to taste

Combine all the ingredients in a bowl and mix thoroughly. Chill well before serving. In addition to curries, you can serve this with chilies and other spicy dishes.

4 to 6 servings.

In folklore, dreaming of cucumbers had several meanings. If one was ill, a cucumber dream meant a speedy recovery. If one was in love, it meant that marriage was impending. If a sailor dreamt of cucumbers, it meant that his next voyage would be a pleasant one.

SUMMER POTATO SALAD

4 medium potatoes, well scrubbed
2 medium-sized celery stalks, finely
chopped
1 cup steamed fresh or (thawed) frozen
green peas
½ cup minced green pepper
⅓ cup chopped black or green olives
1 bunch scallions, minced
1 tablespoon finely chopped fresh parsley
1 tablespoon minced fresh dill
2 tablespoons toasted sunflower seeds
1 cup plain yogurt or
½ cup plain yogurt and ½ cup sour
cream, mixed
1 to 2 teaspoons Dijon mustard, to taste
Salt and freshly ground pepper to taste
2 hard-boiled eggs, chopped, optional

Cook the potatoes in their skins until tender but still firm. When cool enough to handle, dice them, leaving the skins on, and place them in a large bowl. Allow to cool to room temperature.

Add the remaining ingredients to the potatoes and mix thoroughly. This can be served chilled or at room temperature.

6 servings.

Oh, herbaceous treat!
'Twould tempt the dying anchorite
to eat;
Back to the world he'd turn his
fleeting soul,
And plunge his fingers in the salad
bowl.

—Sydney Smith (1771–1845)
A Receipt for a Salad

After Doré

OPEN SESAME! And while you're at it, bring me some of this sesame salad!

CRISP SESAME VEGETABLES

The sesame dressing and sesame seeds give this crunchy salad a pleasant Oriental accent. This salad enhances Oriental-style egg, rice, or noodle dishes wonderfully.

Choose from among several of the following fresh, raw vegetables:
Bok choy or celery, sliced diagonally
Broccoli florets
Cauliflower florets
Snow peas (you can steam them briefly, if you prefer)
Cabbage, coarsely shredded
Carrot, sliced diagonally
Turnip, peeled and diced
Green pepper, julienned or diced

A good guideline is 5 heaping cups of these vegetables, prepared as described, for 4 large or 6 smaller servings. Combine the vegetables of your choice in a bowl, and add:

1 cup alfalfa sprouts
2 to 3 bunches scallions, chopped

Toss together, separating the sprouts with a fork. Top each serving with:

A generous serving of Tofu Sesame Dressing (page 53)
A sprinkling of sesame seeds

4 to 6 servings.

Say the word "sesame" and it may bring to mind the phrase "Open, Sesame!" which comes to us from the story of "Ali Baba and the Forty Thieves." This magical command enabled Ali Baba to enter the secret cave of treasure.

AVOCADOS STUFFED WITH CURRIED EGG SALAD

Avocados are not only among the most sensuous additions to a salad, but are also a great receptacle for one. This delicious and substantial way to have avocado, with its lovely textures and appealing colors, is high on my list of favorites.

2 large avocados, ripe but not mushy
4 hard-boiled eggs
2 tablespoons minced chives or scallion
1 small carrot, coarsely grated
½ cup plain yogurt or Tofu "Mayonnaise"
 (page 52)
½ cup chopped cucumber
2 tablespoons lemon juice
2 teaspoons good curry powder or
 Home-Mixed Curry (page 170), more or
 less to taste
Salt and freshly ground pepper to taste
Paprika for garnish

Cut the avocados in half lengthwise. Remove the pit and scoop out the pulp, leaving a ¼-inch (⅔ cm) shell all around.

Place the pulp in a mixing bowl and add the eggs, and mash them together with a fork. Add the remaining ingredients and mix together thoroughly. Stuff the avocado halves and sprinkle the paprika over the stuffing.

4 servings.

The ancient Maya and Aztec Indians developed and cultivated many varieties of avocado ages before the Europeans descended upon the Americas. These ancient races evidently had high regard for the avocado, as its depiction is to be found on their pottery and sculpture. The avocado has been known by its native names of ahuacatl *and* aguacate, *as well as the descriptive terms alligator pear and midshipman's butter.*

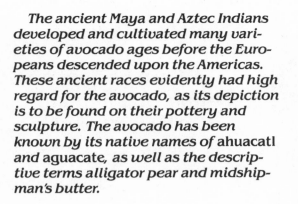

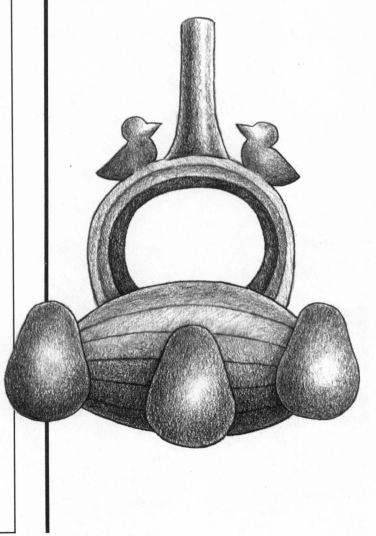

> **"Korn has got one thing that nobody else has got, and that is a kob."**
>
> —Josh Billings
> *His Works, Complete* (1876)

CORN SALAD

Corn is not often used as a salad ingredient, but it is a very pleasant one. This salad goes particularly well with chili-flavored dishes, such as Open-Faced Avocado Bean Tacos (page 86).

4 heaping cups cooked fresh or (thawed) frozen corn kernels
1 cup firmly packed grated zucchini
1/2 cup chopped green olives
1 small sweet red or green pepper, finely chopped
1/3 cup Herb Marinade (page 55)
2 to 3 bunches scallions, finely chopped
2 tablespoons plain yogurt
1/4 teaspoon ground cumin
1/4 teaspoon ground coriander
Salt and freshly ground pepper to taste
2 pickled green chilies, chopped, for garnish, optional

Combine all the ingredients, except the chilies, in a mixing bowl and mix together thoroughly. Chill for 1 hour before serving, garnished with the chilies.

4 to 6 servings.

ITALIAN-STYLE EGGPLANT AND PEPPER SALAD

Eggplant makes a wonderful basis for a salad. Baked whole in its own skin, it develops a deep and slightly smoked flavor. On this page are two distinctive possibilities using this baking method.

1 large eggplant
2 large green peppers, or 1 green pepper and 1 sweet red pepper
2 large celery stalks
Olive or vegetable oil for sautéing
2 cloves garlic, minced
1/4 cup olive oil
1/4 cup red wine vinegar
1 teaspoon dried oregano
Salt and freshly ground pepper to taste
1/4 cup chopped black olives, optional

Preheat the oven to 400°F (205°C).

Place the whole, unpeeled eggplant right on the rack in the hot oven. Wrap the 2 peppers and 2 stalks of celery individually in aluminum foil and place them on the oven rack as well. Bake for 30 minutes, or until the peppers are easily pierced with a fork. Remove them and the celery and allow them to cool. Bake the eggplant another 15 minutes or so, or until it is very tender and has collapsed.

When the vegetables are cool enough to handle, peel the eggplant, cut it into several pieces and allow it to drain in a colander for about 20 minutes, then squeeze out some of the excess moisture. Chop the peppers, removing the stems and seeds; leave them in rather large pieces. Chop the celery into 1/2-inch (1½ cm) pieces. Chop the eggplant into small dice and combine it in a serving bowl with the peppers and celery.

Heat a few drops of oil in a small skillet and sauté the garlic until it is golden. Add to the vegetable mixture along with the remaining ingredients and mix thoroughly. Cover and let stand at room temperature for 1 hour before serving. This is best served at room temperature.

6 or more servings.

MIDDLE EASTERN EGGPLANT SALAD

This version of the Middle Eastern classic is a great favorite with anyone who loves eggplant. It may also be served as an hors d'ouevre dip to be scooped up with pita bread or crackers.

2 medium eggplants (about 2½ pounds, 1,125g)
2 tablespoons olive oil
1 medium onion, chopped
2 to 3 cloves garlic, minced
3 tablespoons finely chopped fresh parsley
Juice of 1/2 lemon
1/4 cup plain yogurt
2 tablespoons tahini (sesame paste)
Salt and freshly ground pepper to taste
2 hard-boiled eggs, chopped, optional

Preheat the oven to 400°F (205°C). Place the whole, unpeeled eggplants right on the oven's rack and bake for approximately 40 minutes, or until the skin is parched and the eggplant is very tender and has collapsed.

Remove from the oven and allow to cool until it can be easily handled.

Heat the olive oil in a skillet. When hot, sauté the onion and garlic over moderately low heat until the onion is translucent. Add the parsley and continue to sauté until the onion and garlic are lightly browned.

Remove and discard the skin from the eggplant and cut each into several smaller pieces. Place in a colander and squeeze out some of the moisture. Transfer the eggplant to a mixing bowl and mash to the desired consistency (some like it almost puréed; I prefer to leave it a little chunkier).

Add the remaining ingredients and mix well. Serve garnished with fresh raw vegetables, such as tomatoes, green peppers, cucumbers, black olives, and extra parsley.

6 to 8 servings.

TABOULEH

On these two pages are a variety of salads made with grains. Grains give texture, substance, and protein as a salad base, but aren't heavy. Tabouleh is a grain salad using bulgur, and is of Middle Eastern origins. It has become quite a vegetarian classic over the past few years.

1 cup raw bulgur
2 medium firm, ripe tomatoes, chopped
1 cup chopped cucumber
1¹/₃ cups cooked or canned chick-peas (about ¹/₂ cup raw, cooked following the directions on page 179)
¹/₄ to ¹/₂ cup chopped fresh parsley, or to taste
2 to 3 bunches finely chopped scallions
2 to 3 tablespoons minced fresh mint leaves or 2 teaspoons dried mint
¹/₄ cup olive oil
Juice of 1 large lemon
Salt and freshly ground pepper to taste

Prepare the bulgur according to directions in Cooking Grains (page 178). Allow it to cool somewhat, then add the remaining ingredients. Mix thoroughly and chill for 1 to 2 hours before serving.

4 to 6 servings.

"Bread, wine, and wholesome salads you may buy. What nature adds besides, is luxury. "

—Horace

BARLEY PILAF SALAD

The combination of barley with beans and yogurt makes for a high protein grain salad with a refreshing, lightly marinated flavor.

³/₄ cup raw barley
2 tablespoons soy sauce or tamari
1 bay leaf
1¹/₂ cups cooked or canned navy or small white beans (about ¹/₂ to ²/₃ cup raw, cooked following the directions on page 179)
¹/₂ medium cucumber, peeled and diced
1 cup steamed string beans, cut into 1-inch (2¹/₂ cm) pieces
¹/₃ cup sliced or chopped black olives
2 tablespoons minced scallion or chives
2 tablespoons minced fresh parsley
¹/₂ cup plain yogurt
¹/₄ cup olive oil
¹/₄ cup red wine vinegar
¹/₂ teaspoon dried basil
¹/₂ teaspoon dried marjoram
¹/₂ teaspoon dried dill
Salt and freshly ground pepper to taste

Cook the barley according to directions in Cooking Grains (page 178), adding the soy sauce and bay leaf to the cooking water. Once the barley is done, remove the bay leaf and allow the barley to cool to room temperature.

Transfer the barley to a mixing bowl. Add the beans, cucumber, string beans, olives, scallions and parsley and mix well.

Combine the remaining ingredients in a small bowl and mix thoroughly. Pour over the salad and toss until everything is evenly coated. You can serve this immediately or let it stand an hour or so at room temperature or refrigerated.

6 servings.

NUTTY BROWN RICE SALAD

1 cup raw brown rice
1 cup chopped nuts, such as almonds,
    walnuts, cashews, peanuts, etc.
1 bunch scallions, finely chopped
1 cup chopped cucumber
1 small green pepper, finely chopped
½ cup alfalfa sprouts
1 tablespoon soy sauce or tamari
Juice of ½ lemon
Freshly ground pepper to taste
½ teaspoon ground cumin
¾ cup plain yogurt, mixed with 1 teaspoon
    Dijon mustard, or ¾ cup Tofu Dijon
    "Mayonnaise" (page 52), or Tofu Garlic
    "Mayonnaise" (page 52), or Tofu
    Sesame Dressing (page 53)

Cook the rice according to directions on page 178 and allow it to cool to room temperature.

Combine the first 6 ingredients in a mixing bowl and toss together. In a small bowl, combine the soy sauce, lemon juice, pepper and cumin with the yogurt and Dijon mustard or the tofu dressing of your choice. Mix well, pour over the salad, and toss together thoroughly.

4 to 6 servings.

> **"***My salad days, when I was green in judgement.* ,,**

—William Shakespeare
Antony and Cleopatra (ca. 1607)

SAUCES AND DRESSINGS

" *Homer has not, if I remember correctly, ever said a word about sauces.* "

—Plato (ca. 427–347 B.C.)

Once relegated to the realms of gourmet cookery, making good sauces and dressings can be a very simple and basic task. Just about every sauce and dressing in this chapter can be made in minutes, and can give new life to an otherwise uninspired dish or even add a new dimension to leftovers.

The dictionary tells us that sauce, as a verb, means "to add zest to," and that the word "sauce" also gives us "saucy," meaning, alternatively, "pert" or "impudent." This interpretation aside, sauce must be associated with something worth reaching for, as we are told that "what is sauce for the goose is sauce for the gander."

A Saucy Little Girl

❝ Sauce: The one infallible sign of civilization and enlightenment. A people with no sauces has one thousand vices; a people with one sauce has only nine hundred and ninety nine. For every sauce invented and accepted a vice is renounced and forgiven. **❞**

—Ambrose Bierce (1842–1914)

BASIC CHINESE SAUCE

You will see this sauce called for in several Oriental style recipes throughout the book. If you are cutting any of these recipes in half, cut this sauce also, making only as much as you need, since it does not keep well on its own.

1 tablespoon sesame oil
2 to 3 cloves garlic, minced
1½ cups vegetable stock or water, or a combination
4 tablespoons soy sauce or tamari, more or less to taste
3 tablespoons dry sherry
½ to 1 teaspoon freshly grated ginger, or to taste
2½ tablespoons cornstarch

Heat the sesame oil in a heavy saucepan. When it is hot, add the garlic and sauté over low heat until it is golden.

For the vegetable stock, use any liquid from canned Chinese vegetables you may be using, such as bamboo shoots or baby corn, or from the sources recommended in Soups (page 12). Make up whatever difference there is with water to equal 1½ cups. Pour the stock over the garlic, then add the soy sauce, sherry, and ginger. Turn the heat to moderate.

Dissolve the cornstarch in a little cold water. When the liquid in the saucepan is just under the boiling point, lower the heat and whisk in the cornstarch. Let the sauce boil slowly until it has thickened, stirring almost continuously.

Makes enough sauce for recipes with 4 to 6 servings.

Variations:

SWEET AND SOUR SAUCE

In the sweet and sour variation of Buddha's Delight (page 131), canned, unsweetened pineapple is recommended if fresh is unavailable. If you use canned, include the liquid in the 1½ cups as well as ¼ cup white or rice vinegar, plus 2 tablespoons honey. If you don't have the pineapple juice, include the ¼ cup vinegar in the 1½ cups liquid, plus the 2 tablespoons honey, then add more honey to taste.

"HOT AND SPICY" SAUCE

Simply add chili oil (available at Oriental groceries) or cayenne pepper or crushed red pepper flakes to taste.

WHITE CHEESE SAUCE

This multipurpose sauce is called for in several of the recipes; it is quick and practically goof-proof.

1 cup firmly packed grated mild white cheese (mozzarella, muenster, or Monterey Jack are good)
2½ tablespoons unbleached white flour
1⅓ cups milk
2 tablespoons butter
½ teaspoon salt

Before starting the sauce, have the grated cheese ready and set aside. Place the flour into a small bowl or cup and mix into it just enough cold water to form a smooth, flowing paste.

In a small saucepan, warm the milk, butter, and salt over moderately low heat. When just under the boiling point, whisk in the cheese, a little at a time. Then, whisk in the flour paste, and continue to whisk until the sauce is smooth and thick.

Variation:
CURRY CHEESE SAUCE

Simply stir 2 teaspoons of good curry powder or Home-Mixed Curry (page 170), more or less to taste, into the White Cheese Sauce as soon as it is done.

ONION AND GARLIC SAUCE

I can promise you that this flavorful sauce will not spoil your kissing, but in fact may improve it since onions and garlic are reputed to be aphrodisiacs. This is especially good served over green vegetables, such as string beans and broccoli.

3 tablespoons unbleached white flour
2 tablespoons butter
2 large onions, chopped
4 large cloves garlic, minced
3 tablespoons soy sauce or tamari
1 tablespoon dry red wine
Pinch of freshly ground pepper

Dissolve the flour in just enough water to form a smooth, flowing paste. Set aside until needed.

In a heavy saucepan, heat the butter until it foams, then add 1 tablespoon water and the onions and garlic. Sauté over very low heat until they are lightly browned, stirring frequently. Stir in 1¼ cups water, raise the heat, and bring to a boil. Add the tamari, the wine, and pepper. Lower the heat and simmer for 5 minutes.

Whisk the flour paste into the sauce, a little at a time. Allow the sauce to boil slowly until it has thickened.

This is ev'ry Cooks Opinion,
No sav'ry Dish without an Onyon;
But lest your kissing should be spoyl'd,
Your Onyons must be th'roughly boyl'd...

—Jonathan Swift (1667–1745)

WHITE BEAN DIP

A nice change of pace from the usual party dips, this subtly spiced, high-protein dip is good for raw vegetables, pita wedges, or unusual crackers.

2 tablespoons olive oil
1/2 medium green pepper, chopped
1 large celery stalk, chopped
1 to 2 cloves garlic, minced
1 1/2 cups cooked or canned white beans,
    such as great northern, navy, or soy
    (about 2/3 cup raw, cooked following
    the directions on page 179)
1/2 teaspoon dried summer savory
1/2 teaspoon chili powder
1/2 teaspoon dried basil
1/4 teaspoon ground cumin
1/4 teaspoon ground coriander
1/2 teaspoon Dijon mustard
1/4 cup plain yogurt
1 teaspoon red wine vinegar
Salt and freshly ground pepper to taste

Heat the olive oil in a skillet. When it is hot, add the green pepper, celery, and garlic. Sauté, covered, over low heat, stirring occasionally, until the vegetables are tender and browned.

Combine the beans, sautéed vegetables, and the remaining ingredients in the workbowl of a food processor or blender and process until smooth.

"*There are in England sixty different religious sects, but only one sauce.***"**

—Francesco Caraccioli (1752-1799)

AVOCADO-TAHINI DIP

Tahini is an unexpected flavor complement to avocado in this rich dip, and an interesting change of pace from guacamole for using your ripe avocados.

1 large, ripe avocado, peeled and diced
1/3 cup sesame paste (tahini)
Juice of 1 lemon
1/2 cup milk
Salt and freshly ground pepper to taste
2 tablespoons minced fresh parsley or
    cilantro, optional

You can make this in a blender or food processor by placing all the ingredients except the parsley or cilantro in the workbowl and processing until smooth. Pour into a serving bowl and stir in the parsley or cilantro.

To make this by hand, put the avocado in a mixing bowl and mash thoroughly. Add the remaining ingredients and stir until well mixed.

Serve with crisp tortillas, pita bread, or raw vegetables.

OLIVE-TAHINI SAUCE

This rich sauce is a tasty way to dress up leftover grains, beans (or a combination of both), and steamed green vegetables.

2 tablespoons unbleached white flour
1 cup milk
¼ cup liquid from canned black olives
⅓ cup sesame paste (tahini)
1 cup finely chopped black olives
Juice of 1 lemon
¼ teaspoon dried thyme
Freshly ground pepper to taste

Dissolve the flour in just enough water to make a smooth, flowing paste. Set aside until needed. Heat the milk and olive liquid slowly in a heavy saucepan. When just under the boiling point, whisk in the tahini, a little at a time, then the flour paste. Simmer over very low heat until the sauce is thick. Stir in the olives, lemon juice, thyme, and pepper, and serve immediately.

> *There is not now a rebel's sword unsheath'd*
> *But peace puts forth her Olive everywhere.*

—William Shakespeare
  Henry IV, ca. 1597

PEANUT SAUCE

Use this as a change-of-pace sauce for stir-fries, noodle or rice dishes, or see an unusual way to use it in Eggs and Tofu in Peanut Sauce (page 62).

½ cup peanut butter
3 to 4 tablespoons soy sauce or tamari
1 small onion, chopped
1 teaspoon freshly grated ginger
2 tablespoons honey
3 tablespoons rice vinegar or white
    vinegar
2 tablespoons dry sherry
1 teaspoon chili powder
Cayenne pepper to taste
½ cup vegetable stock or water

Place all the ingredients in the workbowl of a food processor or blender. Process until smooth. Pour the sauce into a small heavy saucepan and heat over low heat until warm.

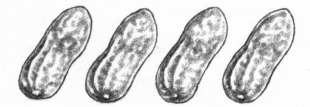

TOFU "MAYONNAISE"

Bean curd, or soy curd, is becoming more commonly known by its Japanese name of tofu, and is a cheese of sorts made from soy milk. It is already well known for its high protein and low fat content, and blended, its texture is excellent for making sauces and dressings. This is a creamy dressing with the consistancy of mayonnaise, with far fewer calories and a lighter, less oily flavor. Use wherever you might use mayonnaise, or as a high-protein salad dressing. Tofu "mayonnaise" will keep in the refrigerator for up to a week.

2 cakes tofu (bean curd)
3 tablespoons safflower or vegetable oil
½ cup plain yogurt
Juice of ½ lemon
½ teaspoon salt
1 egg yolk, optional

Place all the ingredients in the workbowl of a food processor or blender. Process to a velvety texture.

This may also be used as a sauce over grains, and you can vary it in the following ways:

TOFU DIJON MAYONNAISE

Add 1 to 2 teaspoons, to taste, of Dijon mustard before blending.

TOFU GARLIC MAYONNAISE

Sauté 3 cloves of minced garlic until golden and add before blending.

TOFU SESAME DRESSING OR SAUCE

Not only does this give a pleasant, Oriental flavor to salads, but this versatile blend is also a nice way to enhance leftover grains or noodles when warmed up together with them.

2 cakes tofu (bean curd)
⅓ cup tahini (sesame paste)
1 tablespoon sesame oil
1 to 2 cloves garlic, crushed or minced
3 tablespoons rice vinegar or white
**   vinegar**
½ cup vegetable stock or water
¼ cup soy sauce or tamari
2 tablespoons honey
½ teaspoon freshly grated ginger, or to
**   taste**
Pinch of cayenne pepper

Place all the ingredients in the workbowl of a food processor or blender and process until completely smooth.

If you'd like a less pronounced garlic flavor, sauté the garlic in a small amount of oil until golden before processing.

There are three bean curd gods in Chinese folklore. They are Chiao Kuan, whose role is obscure, Huai Nan Tzu, who invented bean curd, and Kuan Yu, depicted here, who was a bean curd seller when he was young, and grew up to be the great war god.

Herbs, too, she knew, and well of
    each could speak
That in her garden sip'd the silv'ry
    dew;
Where no vain flow'r disclosed a
    gaudy streak
But herbs for use, and physic, not a
    few,
Of grey renown within these
    borders grew...

—William Shenstone (1714—1764)
    "The School Mistress"

GREEN HERB SAUCE

*Herbs add the flavor interest to this and the
remaining recipes in this chapter. If you can use any or
all fresh herbs, so much the better; substitute using a 3
to 1 ratio.*

2½ tablespoons unbleached white flour
1⅓ cups milk
1 tablespoon butter
½ teaspoon salt
½ teaspoon dried dill
½ teaspoon dried summer savory
½ teaspoon dried basil
¼ teaspoon dried oregano
¼ teaspoon dried marjoram
½ cup sour cream or plain yogurt
2 hard-boiled eggs, chopped, optional

Dissolve the flour in just enough water to make
a smooth, flowing paste. Set aside until needed.

In a heavy saucepan, heat the milk, butter, and
salt slowly. While they are heating, stir in the
herbs. When just under the boiling point, whisk in
the flour paste. Allow the sauce to boil slowly, and
stir constantly until it has thickened.

Remove from the heat and let stand for 30 seconds or so, then stir in the sour cream or yogurt
and the chopped eggs. Serve immediately over
freshly steamed vegetables or leftover grains.

Come sweetheart, come,
Dear as my heart to me,
Come to the room
I have made fine for thee.
Here be the couches spread
Tapestries tented,
Flowers for thee to tread,
Green herbs, sweet scented.

—Medieval Love Song

HERB MARINADE

This is a basic dressing for marinating steamed or parboiled vegetables, or simply as an Italian-style salad dressing, with a little less oil and more pungency than a vinaigrette.

½ cup olive oil, or ¼ cup olive oil and ¼ cup vegetable or safflower oil
½ cup red wine vinegar
½ teaspoon Dijon mustard
2 to 2½ teaspoons mixed dried herbs (choose from several among oregano, dill, marjoram, savory, basil, thyme, tarragon)
Freshly ground pepper to taste

Combine all the ingredients in a jar with a tight-fitting lid or cruet and shake well.

YOGURT-DILL DRESSING

Yogurt has been around for millenia, though its exact origins are unclear. Yogurt, now well known for its great nutritive values, is fermented from milk by live cultures and is a staple food for several societies renowned for their longevity. Methusela, who is famous for supposedly having lived for 900 years, was reportedly a big fan of yogurt. Likewise, the wise King Solomon enjoyed it, and it was a great favorite of the biblical patriarch Abraham, who was fond of goat's milk yogurt. Genghis Khan, the Mongol conqueror, ate great quantities of it, and his preference was a yak's milk yogurt.

This quick and simple dressing is very refreshing with any mixed green salad.

1 cup plain yogurt
¼ cup olive oil
**2 to 3 tablespoons minced fresh dill, or 1
    to 1½ tablespoons dried dill**
Juice of ½ lemon

Combine all the ingredients in a small bowl and mix until thoroughly blended.

CUCUMBER-SCALLION DRESSING

John Evelyn, a seventeenth-century writer, said of cucumbers that "…the pulp in broth is greatly refreshing, and may be mingl'd in most sallets." Combined with a "broth" of yogurt, another great refresher, cucumbers make an excellent base for a light and low-calorie dressing.

1 medium cucumber, peeled and chopped
2 bunches scallions
¼ cup safflower or vegetable oil
½ cup plain yogurt
Juice of ½ lemon
½ teaspoon dried tarragon, optional
¼ teaspoon dried summer savory
¼ teaspoon dried basil
Freshly ground pepper to taste

Place all the ingredients in the workbowl of a food processor or blender and process until smooth.

PARSLEY DRESSING

This pale green dressing, with tiny specks of darker green, tastes as refreshing as it looks. A little goes a long way.

1 cup firmly packed fresh parsley
¼ cup vegetable or safflower oil
¼ cup olive oil
½ cup chopped cucumber
2 tablespoons lemon juice
1 teaspoon dried dill
½ teaspoon salt
Freshly ground pepper to taste

Place all the ingredients in the workbowl of a food processor or blender. Process until all that remains of the parsley are tiny flakes.

" *There is no garden hearb comes neare unto parsley, as well for toothsomenesse as for health.* **"**

—William Vaughn
Directions for Health (1617)

57

EGGS AND CHEESES

"Don't touch me please," she said softly. *"I am part egg-shell. Or perhaps I had better put it in a safe place."* She began unfastening the collar of her gown.

"What is it?" said her lover.

"An egg—a Cochin's egg. I am hatching a very rare sort. I carry it everywhere with me, and it will get hatched in less than three weeks."

"Where do you carry it?"

"Just here." She put her hand into her bosom and drew out the egg…

—Thomas Hardy
Jude the Obscure (1885)

59

The egg, apart from its many culinary and nutritive merits, has a legacy richer than any other food item. Eggs are somehow mysterious and have been the objects of numerous folktales, riddles, and rhymes, whether portrayed as immeasurably precious, as in The Goose That Laid the Golden Egg, or as irreparably damaged, as in "Humpty Dumpty." From the most ancient times, eggs have been symbolic of the soul, the earth, and of life itself, as the embodiment of the new birth.

In religious rites in the western world, eggs play an important role in the Easter celebration of Christians and the Passover feast of the Jews. Eggs have also played a role in fertility rites. Arabella Donne, whom we have seen on the preceding page, was attempting to seduce Jude so that he would impregnate her (and thereby have to marry her), and the egg ritual was a way of ensuring her fertility. For similar ends, seventeenth-century French brides broke an egg upon entering their new homes. To others, eggs have meant abundance, as they did to Slavs of days past, who would smear their plows with a mixture of eggs, bread, and flour in hopes of a plentiful harvest.

Eggs are one of the foods mentioned most frequently as aphrodisiacs. Their power to arouse has been written of in many volumes, including the Kama Sutra, The Perfumed Garden, the writings of Ovid, and Tacuinum Sanitatis (Medieval Health Handbook), which praises ordinary eggs as having the ability to "increase coitus noticeably."

Aside from being decorated and bejeweled themselves, eggs have adorned the prose, poetry, wit, and wisdom of writers both ancient and modern. This chapter holds but a very small sampling of the literature and lore of the marvelous and mysterious egg.

BAKED EGGS AND CHEESE WITH VEGETABLES

A good way to use up odds and ends of vegetables you may have on hand, this is bound to please even the most grumpy palate.

Choose from among the following vegetables:

string beans	asparagus
zucchini	sweet red or green
broccoli	peppers
cauliflower	corn kernels
carrots	peas
mushrooms	

Use 4 to 6 different vegetables, cut into bite-sized pieces, and steam or stir-fry them until they are done to a firm texture. Fresh vegetables are of course preferable; frozen corn kernels and peas are fine if thawed in advance. You can use anywhere from 4 to 6 cups of cooked vegetables.

2 tablespoons butter
1 large onion, chopped
8 eggs, well beaten
1/3 cup milk
Salt and freshly ground pepper to taste
1 to 2 teaspoons mixed dried herbs (such as dill, marjoram, thyme, basil, etc.)
2 cups grated cheese of your choice
Sesame seeds or wheat germ for topping

Preheat the oven to 350°F (180°C).

Heat the butter in a small skillet until it foams. Add the onion and sauté over moderate heat until it is lightly browned.

In a large mixing bowl, combine the beaten eggs with the milk; add salt and pepper. Combine your cooked vegetables with the sautéed onion in a separate bowl and season them with salt and pepper and the herbs of your choice.

Oil a large, deep casserole and layer as follows: one third of the eggs, one third of the vegetables, and one third of the cheese; repeat twice. Sprinkle the top with sesame seeds or wheat germ. Bake for 35 to 40 minutes, or until eggs are set and the top is lightly browned.

4 to 6 servings.

SPROUTY EGG "CRÊPES"

These chewy, Oriental-flavored "crêpes" are a nice accompaniment (and a good protein supplement) to freshly steamed or stir-fried vegetables with rice.

1 tablespoon sesame oil
2 cloves garlic, peeled and minced
2 celery stalks, finely chopped
2 tablespoons soy sauce or tamari
2 2/3 cups firmly packed alfalfa sprouts
2 tablespoons wheat germ
8 eggs
8 tablespoons milk
Freshly ground pepper
Butter for frying

Heat the sesame oil in a large skillet. When the oil is hot, add the garlic and celery and sauté over moderately low heat until the vegetables are golden. If you need extra moisture in the skillet, add a tablespoon or two of water. Add the soy sauce and the alfalfa sprouts, separating them with a fork, and sauté just until the sprouts are a bit wilted. Stir in the wheat germ and remove from heat.

Set your oven at 450°F (230°C) or turn on your broiler.

To prepare the eggs, you will need a 6-or 7-inch (15 or 18 cm) skillet, preferably a nonstick, Silverstone type. Beat 1 egg at a time in a small bowl with 1 tablespoon of milk and a little pepper. Melt just enough butter to coat the bottom of the skillet. When it is hot enough to make a drop of egg sizzle, pour it in, and tip the pan to distribute it. Keep tipping, lifting the edges of the egg with a spatula so the loose egg runs underneath. When the bottom is lightly browned and the top is fairly set, flip and let the second side brown lightly. Slide it out and repeat with each remaining egg.

Place a bit of the sprouts mixture down the center of each crêpe. Fold one side over the other and secure with a toothpick. Arrange in a buttered or oiled baking dish and place in the oven or under the broiler for 3 to 5 minutes, or until piping hot. Serve with extra soy sauce or tamari.

4 servings.

EGGS AND TOFU IN PEANUT SAUCE

This peanut-flavored egg and tofu combination is excellent served as a small, protein-packed side portion to vegetable stir-fries such as Buddha's Delight (page 130).

1 cup Peanut Sauce (page 52)
Butter for frying
6 eggs, well beaten
2 cakes tofu (bean curd)
1 tablespoon sesame oil
3 bunches scallions
3 tablespoons sunflower seeds
1 16-ounce (450g) can Chinese straw
mushrooms, drained (save the liquid
for future use, or for making the
Peanut Sauce)
Extra soy sauce or tamari to taste,
optional

Prepare the Peanut Sauce according to the recipe. You will only need one cup of it for this; the rest can be saved for leftover grains or vegetables. Set aside.

Heat just enough butter to coat the bottom of an 8- or 9-inch (20 or 23 cm) skillet, preferably a nonstick Silverstone type. When it is very hot and foamy, pour in half the beaten eggs. Tip the pan as you would for an omelet, allowing the loose egg to run underneath. When the bottom is lightly browned and the top is fairly set, flip with a wide spatula and fry for just a minute or so. Remove to a plate and repeat with the remaining eggs. Cut the eggs into 1- by 2-inch (2½ by 5 cm) strips. Slice the tofu so that it resembles the eggs.

Heat the sesame oil in the same skillet. When hot, add the scallions and sunflower seeds and sauté over moderately low heat until the scallion is wilted and the seeds are lightly toasted. Add the remaining ingredients and sauté, stirring gently, until just heated through.

4 to 6 servings.

Note: If you are unable to find straw mushrooms, substitute a cup or so of sliced fresh mushrooms. Add them at the same time as the scallions and seeds.

EASY EGGS FOO YONG

A great vehicle for lots of fresh bean sprouts, try serving this with Cold Sesame Noodles (page 111) and Sunflower Coleslaw (page 35) for an unusual Oriental meal.

1 recipe Basic Chinese Sauce (page 48)
2 tablespoons sesame oil
1 tablespoon soy sauce or tamari
4 cups (about 1 pound, 450g) fresh mung
bean sprouts
4 bunches scallions, chopped
½ pound (225g) mushrooms, sliced
8 eggs
Freshly ground pepper to taste
Oil for frying

Prepare the sauce according to recipe, just up to the point before heating it and set aside.

Heat the sesame oil and soy sauce in a large skillet or wok. When hot, add the bean sprouts, scallions, and mushrooms and stir-fry over moderate heat just until they have lost their raw quality. The sprouts should still be quite crisp but slightly wilted. Remove from the heat.

Beat 2 of the eggs in a small bowl. Add to them a little freshly ground pepper and one quarter of the stir-fried vegetables, and mix well. Heat just enough oil to coat the bottom of a 6- or 7-inch (15 or 18 cm) skillet, preferably a nonstick, Silverstone type. When very hot, pour in the egg and vegetable mixture, turn the heat to moderately low, cover, and fry until the bottom is nicely browned and the eggs are fairly set on top. Flip with a wide spatula and brown the other side, uncovered. Repeat the process with every 2 eggs. While the last pancake is frying, finish preparing the sauce.

Makes 4 pancakes; each pancake is one serving. If you're not following the menu suggestion above, you can serve these over rice. In either case, top each serving with a generous helping of sauce.

> **"A hen is only an egg's way of making another egg. "**
>
> —Samuel Butler
> *Life and Habit* (1877)

CURRIED EGGS

This is an easy and versatile dish that can be served over toast, rice, noodles, or on its own with vegetable curries.

1 tablespoon butter
1 medium-sized sweet red or green pepper, cut into julienne strips
2 tablespoons chopped cilantro or fresh parsley
1 recipe Curry Cheese Sauce (page 49)
A pinch or two of cayenne pepper
¼ teaspoon ground turmeric, optional
Salt to taste
8 large hard-boiled eggs, thinly sliced

Heat the butter in a small skillet until it foams. Add the red or green pepper and sauté until tender but not brown. Add the cilantro or parsley and sauté until they are slightly wilted. Remove from the heat.

Stir the sautéed peppers, herbs, and seasonings into the Curry Cheese Sauce. Gently fold in the eggs and cook over low heat until nicely heated through.

4 servings.

Behold the fool saith, "Put not all thine eggs in one basket," but the wise man saith, "Put all your eggs in one basket—and watch that basket!"

—Mark Twain
Pudd'nhead Wilson (1894)

> **"** *Be content to remember that those who can make omelettes properly can do nothing else. And thank the Lord that you have other talents... There is nothing made by man, no, not even his false religions, which for full success requires so complete a conduct of the affair as the making of an omelette.* **"**

—Hilaire Belloc
A Conversation with a Cat (1931)

Since it's a bit difficult to make and keep warm four or more omelets, as they are made one at a time and should be eaten as soon as possible thereafter, the recipes on these two pages provide for two omelets, albeit substantial ones. That being the case, these are appropriate for an intimate dinner for someone you may be about to fall in love with, or someone you are in love with already. All you need to complete these meals is a good bread, an interesting salad, white wine, and a fruity dessert.

HERBED POTATO-BRIE OMELET

1 large potato, cooked or baked in its skin
1 tablespoon safflower or vegetable oil
1 small onion, minced
2 tablespoons minced fresh parsley
1 tablespoon minced fresh dill or 1
    teaspoon dried dill
1/2 teaspoon paprika
1/2 teaspoon dried marjoram
1/2 teaspoon dried basil
Salt and freshly ground pepper to taste
4 eggs
2 tablespoons milk
2 tablespoons butter
1/4 pound (115g) Brie, sliced thin and
    divided in half

Peel and slice the cooked or baked potato when cool enough to handle. Heat the oil in a large skillet. When hot, add the onion and sauté over moderate heat until translucent. Add 2 tablespoons of water to the skillet. Then add the potato and continue to sauté until both the onion and potato are lightly browned. Add the parsley and other seasonings, stir together, and remove from the heat.

Break 2 eggs each into 2 separate bowls and add 1 tablespoon of milk to each. Beat the eggs until bubbly.

The easiest way to make a good omelet if you're not an expert with a well seasoned omelet pan is to use an 8- or 9-inch (20 or 23 cm) Silverstone skillet. Melt 1 tablespoon of the butter over moderate heat. When it is very foamy, swirl it around the pan, then test with a drop of water. If it really sizzles, pour in one of the bowls full of beaten eggs.

Tip the pan so that the eggs coat the skillet evenly. Keep tipping occasionally, lifting the omelet's edge so that the loose egg runs underneath. When the eggs are fairly set on top, but still moist, quickly arrange half the potato mixture on one side of the omelet or in the middle third, followed by half the Brie slices. Fold the omelet in half or fold the outside edges over the middle, according to where you arranged the potato mixture. Slide the omelet out onto a plate and cover carefully with foil or a matching plate to keep it warm while repeating the process with the second omelet.

Makes 2 omelets.

PERFUMED GARDEN ASPARAGUS OMELET

3 tablespoons butter
1 clove garlic, minced
2 medium firm, ripe tomatoes, finely
    chopped
2 tablespoons minced fresh parsley or
    cilantro
4 tablespoons grated Parmesan cheese
¼ teaspoon dried basil
½ pound asparagus, cut into 1-inch (2½
    cm) pieces and steamed tender-crisp
Salt and freshly ground pepper to taste
4 eggs
2 tablespoons milk
1 teaspoon good curry powder or
    Home-Mixed Curry (page 170)

Heat 1 tablespoon of the butter in a skillet until it foams. Add the garlic and sauté over low heat until it is golden. Add the tomatoes and sauté until they soften, but do not reduce them. Add the parsley, the Parmesan cheese, basil, the steamed asparagus, and salt and pepper. Remove from the heat and cover.

Break 2 eggs each into 2 separate bowls and add 1 tablespoon of milk to each. Beat the eggs until bubbly, then stir ½ teaspoon of the curry into each bowl.

Use the remaining butter, 1 tablespoon for each omelet, following the directions for preparation as in the previous recipe, stuffing them with half the asparagus mixture each.

Makes 2 omelets.

"He who boils asparagus, and then fries them in fat, and then pours upon them the yolks of eggs with pounded condiments, and eats every day of this dish, will grow very strong for coitus, and find in it a stimulant for his amorous desires. **"**

—Shaykh Nefzawi
The Perfumed Garden (ca. 1400)

FRITTATA OF PEPPERS AND FINE NOODLES

A frittata sounds fancy, but it is quite simply a flat omelet. Precede this with Avocado Gazpacho (page 12), add some good bread and some crisp raw vegetables, and you've got a light summer supper—or lunch, for that matter.

2 heaping cups raw fine egg noodles
2 tablespoons olive oil
1 medium onion, chopped
1 large sweet red pepper, cut into julienne strips
1 large green pepper, cut into julienne strips
2 medium ripe tomatoes, chopped
6 eggs, well beaten
½ cup small curd cottage cheese or ricotta cheese
1 teaspoon paprika
½ teaspoon dried oregano
¼ teaspoon chili powder
Salt and freshly ground pepper to taste

Cook the noodles *al dente*—they need to be extra firm for this, so watch them carefully. Drain and set aside.

Heat the olive oil in a skillet. When hot, add the onion and sauté over moderately low heat until translucent. Add the peppers and tomatoes and sauté until the peppers are tender-crisp and the tomatoes are quite reduced.

In a mixing bowl, combine the beaten eggs with the cottage or ricotta cheese. Add the noodles, peppers mixture, and the seasonings and mix thoroughly.

Divide into 2 parts and prepare following the directions on page 180 for "How to Fry and Flip a Skillet Pie or Frittata."

Makes 2 frittatas, about 4 servings. Each half of 1 frittata makes a light but substantial main portion.

EASY CORN FRITTATA

This frittata can be whipped up very quickly. Try serving it with Linguini Aglio Olio (page 104), which is also quick to fix, and a big salad using lots of seasonal vegetables.

1 tablespoon safflower or vegetable oil
1 large onion, chopped
6 eggs, beaten
½ cup milk
3 cups cooked fresh or (thawed) frozen
    corn kernels
½ cup cornmeal or matzo meal
1 cup grated cheese of your choice,
    optional
Salt and freshly ground pepper to taste

Heat the oil in a skillet. When hot, add the onion and sauté over moderate heat until the onion is lightly browned.

In a mixing bowl, beat the eggs well with the milk. Add the remaining ingredients including the sautéed onion and mix well.

Divide the mixture into 2 parts and prepare following the directions on page 180 for "How to Fry and Flip a Skillet Pie or Frittata."

Makes 2 frittatas, about 4 servings. Each half of 1 frittata makes a light but substantial main portion. You can also use this as a side portion by cutting the frittata into wedges to serve.

According to folk-belief, if you dream of eggs it is an omen of luck, money, or marriage.

> *I can't see you tonight — I have a deadline...*

"Promises and Pie-Crust are made to be broken."

—Jonathan Swift (1667–1745)
Polite Conversation

PUFFED SPINACH AND FETA CHEESE QUICHE

Speaking of pie crust, quiches are such a pleasant and relatively easy way to use eggs and cheese that they've almost become a vegetarian cliché. The two versions on these pages hope to get a little off that beaten path. This one, using a quiche standby, spinach, is given a lightness by separating the eggs, and has a nice tang due to the lemon, fresh herbs, and feta cheese.

1 tablespoon butter
1 small onion, finely chopped
1/3 cup minced fresh herbs (combine parsley with small amounts of dill and/or basil)
3/4 pound (340g) spinach, stemmed, well washed, steamed and finely chopped and drained or 1 10-ounce (285g) package frozen chopped spinach, thawed and thoroughly drained
Juice of 1/2 lemon
3 tablespoons milk
1/4 pound (115g) feta cheese, finely crumbled
1 cup grated mild white cheese of your choice
1/2 teaspoon ground cumin
Pinch of nutmeg
Salt and freshly ground pepper to taste
3 eggs, separated
1 regular, unbaked 9-inch (23 cm) pie shell

Preheat the oven to 325°F (165°C).

Heat the butter in a small skillet. When it foams, add the onion and sauté until it is translucent. Add the herbs and sauté only until they are slightly wilted.

In a mixing bowl, combine the onion and herb mixture with the spinach, lemon juice, milk, the two cheeses, and the seasonings. Mix well.

Separate the eggs; stir the yolks into the spinach mixture. Beat the egg whites until they form stiff peaks. Fold gently into the spinach mixture, then pour into the pie shell. Bake for 35 to 40 minutes, or until the quiche is puffed and lightly browned.

4 to 6 servings.

CURRIED QUICHE WITH CHICK-PEAS AND STRING BEANS

Eggs taste wonderful when they're curried, so why not curry a quiche? Chick-peas are certainly an unusual element for a quiche, but they add to the exotic flavor.

1 tablespoon olive oil
1 medium onion, chopped
2 cloves garlic, minced
4 eggs, well beaten
1 tablespoon minced fresh parsley or
       cilantro
1½ cups cooked or canned chick-peas
       (about ⅔ cups raw, cooked following
       the directions on page 179)
1 cup steamed string beans, cut into
       1-inch (2½ cm) pieces
1½ teaspoons good curry powder or
       Home-Mixed Curry (page 170)
¼ teaspoon ground coriander
⅛ teaspoon ground tumeric
⅛ teaspoon dry mustard
Salt and freshly ground pepper to taste
1 regular unbaked 9-inch (23 cm) pie shell
1 cup firmly packed grated mild cheese
Wheat germ and paprika for topping

Preheat the oven to 350°F (180°C).

Heat the olive oil in a small skillet. When it is hot, add the onion and garlic and sauté over moderate heat until they are golden.

In a mixing bowl, combine the beaten eggs with the parsley, chick-peas, string beans, seasonings, and the sautéed onion and garlic. Mix thoroughly. Pour half of this mixture into the pie shell; top with half of the grated cheese. Pour in the remaining mixture, and top with the remaining cheese and sprinkle with wheat germ and paprika.

Bake for 45 minutes, or until the top is golden and the eggs are set. Let the quiche stand for 5 to 10 minutes before serving.

4 to 6 servings.

In marble walls as white as milk,
Lined with a skin as soft as silk;
Within a fountain crystal clear,
A golden apple doth appear.
No doors there are to this
*   stronghold,*
Yet thieves break in and steal the
*   gold.*

—Old English Riddle

It has been supposed that cheese-making originated in the Middle East, and that the first forms of cheese may have been simply curds, similar to cottage cheese—a coagulation of milk solids. Records of cheese-making date back to ancient Egypt, Rome, and Greece. It seems that almost every culture developed its unique way of curing cheese, and rarely did it not hold the status of a delicacy.

"*One cheese differs from another, and the difference is in sweeps, and in landscapes, and in provinces, and in countrysides, and in climates, and in principalities, and in realms, and in the nature of things. Cheese does most gloriously reflect the multitudinous effect of earthly things...*"

—Hilaire Belloc
First and Last (1931)

SWISS CHEESE OR GRUYÈRE PANCAKES

These crêpe-like pancakes are a nice accompaniment to fresh vegetable dishes like Summer Harvest Squash Sauté (page 123). They may also be stuffed with chopped, steamed vegetables, such as spinach or zucchini, or served with a sauce, such as Onion and Garlic Sauce (page 49).

3 eggs, well beaten
1 cup milk
2 tablespoons dry white wine
½ cup unbleached white flour
¼ cup wheat germ
½ teaspoon salt
½ teaspoon paprika
½ teaspoon dry mustard
1 teaspoon caraway seeds, optional
2 cups firmly packed grated Swiss or
**   Gruyère cheese**
Safflower or vegetable oil for frying

In a mixing bowl, combine the beaten eggs with the milk and wine. Stir in the flour, wheat germ, and seasonings, then add the cheese and mix thoroughly.

Heat just enough oil to coat the bottom of a 6- or 7-inch (15 or 18 cm) non-stick Silverstone skillet. When the skillet seems very hot, test it with a drop of batter. If it really sizzles, turn the heat to moderate and pour in about ¼ cup of the batter. Tip the skillet quickly to distribute the batter. Fry until the bottom is nicely browned and the top is fairly set; flip with a wide spatula and brown the other side. The first one may not come out perfectly, but don't be discouraged.

Makes about 10 pancakes, about 2 per serving. If you serve them plain, roll them up and close them securely with a toothpick; if you stuff them or sauce them, fold as you would a crêpe—one side over the other in the center.

VEGETABLE CHEESE KNISHES

This recipe is actually a composite of the Jewish dairy specialty, Cheese Knishes, and a recent vegetarian favorite, Russian Vegetable Pie. Cheese Knishes, relying mainly on ricotta or farmer cheese are a bit bland, and in the standard Russian Vegetable Pie recipe, the cream cheese and heavy crust seem to overpower the subtly seasoned vegetables. Transposing the vegetables into the cheese knishes results in a suitably delicate combination.

1 recipe Potato Dough (page 144)
2 eggs, beaten
2 cups ricotta cheese
1/2 teaspoon salt
2 tablespoons vegetable or safflower oil
1 1/2 cups finely shredded cabbage
1 medium carrot, grated
1 medium onion, finely chopped
4 to 5 medium mushrooms, chopped
1/4 cup beer
1 tablespoon red wine vinegar
2 teaspoons dried dill
1 teaspoon poppy or dill seeds
Salt and freshly ground pepper to taste

Prepare the potato dough as directed in the recipe and let it rest. Preheat the oven to 350°F (180°C).

In a small mixing bowl, combine the beaten eggs with the ricotta and salt. Mix well and set aside.

Heat the oil in a skillet, and when it is hot, add the cabbage, carrot, and onion. Cover and sauté until the onion is translucent. Add the mushrooms, beer, vinegar, and seasonings and cook, covered, until all the liquid has been absorbed and the vegetables are tender-crisp.

Roll the dough out for filling as directed in the Potato Dough recipe. Place about 2 heaping tablespoons of the ricotta mixture in the center of each square of dough, followed by a bit of the vegetable mixture. Fold each corner toward the center, overlapping each just a little, and pinch the corners shut. Arrange on an oiled and floured baking sheet and bake for 35 minutes, or until the dough is lightly browned.

Makes about 10 knishes.

COTTAGE CHEESE BLUEBERRY PANCAKES

These pancakes are quite nice to have for a leisurely weekend breakfast.

4 eggs, well beaten
1/2 cup milk
1 cup small curd cottage cheese
3 tablespoons honey
1/2 cup whole wheat flour
4 tablespoons wheat germ
1 teaspoon cinnamon
1 1/3 cup blueberries (preferably fresh, but frozen may be used if thawed and well drained)
Oil for frying

In a mixing bowl, blend the beaten eggs with the milk, cottage cheese, and honey. Add the flour, half at a time, stirring it in, followed by the wheat germ, cinnamon, and blueberries.

Since this batter is somewhat sticky, you will need a nonstick, 6- or 7-inch (15 or 18 cm) Silverstone skillet. Heat just enough oil, over moderate heat, to coat the bottom of the skillet. When the oil is really hot, turn the heat to moderately low heat (make sure that a drop of the batter sizzles), pour in about 1/4 to 1/3 cup of the batter. Tip the pan so that the batter runs to the sides. When the bottom is brown and the top is fairly firm, flip the pancake with a wide spatula and brown the other side. Don't be discouraged if the first one doesn't come out well; the skillet must be very hot. For each pancake, add a drop of oil to the skillet before starting.

This makes about 10 pancakes, 2 to 3 per serving. Serve with preserves, sour cream, or applesauce.

"*Cheese: Milk's leap toward immortality.*"

—Clifton Fadiman (1904–   )

THE FOX AND THE CROW

A Crow had snatched a goodly piece of cheese out of a window and flew with it into a high tree, intent to enjoy her prize. A Fox spied the dainty morsel, and thus he planned his approaches. "O Crow," said he, "how beautiful are thy wings, how bright thine eye! how graceful thy neck! thy breast is the breast of an eagle! thy claws—I beg pardon—thy talons, are a match for all the beasts of the field. O! that such a bird should be dumb, and want only a voice!" The Crow, pleased with the flattery, and chuckling to think how she would surprise the Fox with her caw, opened her mouth—down dropped the cheese! which the Fox snapping up, observed, as he walked away, "that whatever he had remarked of her beauty, he had said nothing yet of her brains."

Men seldom flatter without some private end in view; and they who listen to such music may expect to have to pay the piper.

—The Fables of Aesop

TOMATO AND ZUCCHINI RAREBIT

An easy cheese and bread dish, this vegetable variation of Welsh Rarebit is zesty and super-quick.

Vegetable or safflower oil or butter for sautéing
1 small onion, minced
1 medium zucchini, grated
2 medium tomatoes, finely chopped
½ pound (225 g) sharp Cheddar cheese, grated or diced
2 tablespoons flour
2 tablespoons butter
2 teaspoons Worcestershire sauce (caution to those who don't eat fish— some Worcestershire sauces contain anchovies)
1 teaspoon dry mustard
A few grains of cayenne pepper
½ cup beer
8 slices warmed whole grain bread

Heat a small amount of oil or butter in a skillet. When it is hot, add the onion and sauté over moderately low heat until the onion is translucent. Add the zucchini and tomatoes and continue to sauté, stirring often, until they soften.

Place the cheese, flour, butter, Worcestershire sauce, mustard, and cayenne in a heavy saucepan. Heat slowly over very low heat, stirring almost constantly, until the cheese has melted. Add the beer, stirring it in until completely blended with the cheese. Add the vegetables and simmer on as low heat as possible for about 2 minutes. Spread 2 slices of the warmed bread on each plate per serving and pour the cheese mixture over them.

4 servings.

Variation: Although Rarebit is traditionally served over bread, you can also serve it over grains or noodles.

CHEESE AND BREAD PUDDING

A tasty and easy combination of cheese, bread, and eggs, this is particularly attractive with freshly steamed vegetables on the side, and an interesting salad such as Italian-Style Eggplant and Pepper Salad (page 43).

2 tablespoons butter
1 medium onion, chopped
1 clove garlic, minced
4 eggs, well beaten
¾ cup milk or light cream
¼ cup dry white wine
6 average slices soft whole grain bread
1½ cups firmly packed grated cheese of
your choice
½ cup grated Parmesan cheese
½ teaspoon Dijon mustard
½ teaspoon paprika
Pinch of cayenne pepper
Salt and freshly ground pepper to taste
1 teaspoon caraway seeds, optional

Preheat the oven to 325° F (165°C).

Heat the butter in a small skillet. When it foams, add the onion and garlic, and sauté over moderately low heat until they are lightly browned.

Beat the eggs in a large mixing bowl until they are bubbly. Stir in the milk and the wine. Tear the bread into small pieces and add it to the egg mixture. Let it soak for about 5 minutes, then add all the remaining ingredients including the onion and garlic and mix thoroughly.

Pour the mixture into an oiled, 9- by 9-inch (23 by 23 cm) casserole dish or a 9-inch (23 cm) round casserole dish and bake for 35 minutes, or until the top is lightly browned.

4 to 6 servings.

> **"*Bachelor's fare:*
> *Bread and cheese,*
> *and kisses. "*
>
> —Jonathan Swift (1667–1745)
> *Polite Conversation*

GRAINS
AND
LEGUMES

Rice, the grain which is the staff of life for half the world's population, has long been part of the wedding ritual in India and China, where it symbolizes abundance, fertility, and life itself. Most likely it was this use of rice in nuptial ceremonies in the East that influenced its adoption by the West. In the late nineteenth century, the practice of throwing rice at the bridal couple had become common both in Victorian England and in the United States. This ritual, having persisted to the present day, is now simply a way of saying "Good Luck" to the newlyweds, sending them off with wishes of happiness.

Grains are the seeds or fruits of the cereal grasses, most of which are immeasurably ancient. That being the case, it is especially curious to note that many grains today are still struggling to emerge as everyday foods rather than just being labeled as "health foods." However, grains are definitely making a comeback, as more and more is being said about their good protein and fiber content and their versatility in cookery. This chapter will present sample recipes using the more common grains. For cooking specifics, see Cooking Grains, page 178.

The word cereal derives from the Latin adjective cerealis, which means "of Ceres." Ceres was the Roman Goddess of the Harvest, the protector and overseer of the crops. Also known as Demeter in Greek mythology, Ceres is closely related in function to the conception of the Egyptian earth mother Isis. By whatever name, this powerful goddess was the benefactress of the fruitful earth and it was her influence that insured the bountiful yield of grain.

HERBED WHEAT BERRIES, BARLEY AND BLACKEYE PEAS

Wheat berries are simply whole wheat—ground, they make whole wheat flour; cracked, they make bulgur. Combining their distinct flavor and texture with those of barley and blackeye peas makes for a very appealing pilaf.

1/2 cup raw wheat berries
1/3 cup raw barley
1/4 cup olive oil
3 to 4 cloves garlic, minced
1 medium onion, finely chopped
1 medium carrot, thinly sliced
1 1/2 cups cooked or canned blackeye peas
 (about 2/3 cup raw, cooked following
 the directions on page 179)
Juice of 1/2 to 1 lemon, to taste
1/4 teaspoon dried summer savory
1/4 teaspoon dried dill
1/4 teaspoon dried basil
1/4 teaspoon dried marjoram
Salt and freshly ground pepper to taste
1/2 cup firmly packed chopped fresh parsley

Cook the wheat berries and barley separately (see Cooking Grains, page 178), until done but still firm.

Heat half the oil in a large skillet. When it is hot, add the garlic, onion, and carrot and sauté over low heat until they are golden.

Add the remaining oil, the blackeye peas, the cooked grains and remaining ingredients except parsley. Sauté over low heat for 10 minutes, stirring frequently. Add the parsley and sauté for 2 minutes or so longer.

6 servings.

BULGUR BROCCOLI PILAF

Bulgur is whole wheat berries that have been pre-steamed and cracked. It is nutty and chewy; a good way to get to know it is to substitute it whenever you'd use rice.

1 cup raw bulgur
2 tablespoons safflower or vegetable oil
2 heaping cups finely chopped broccoli
1 large onion, chopped
2 cloves garlic, minced
1 14-ounce (400 g) can imported plum tomatoes with liquid, chopped
2 cups cooked or canned kidney or red beans or chick-peas (about ¾ cup raw, cooked following the directions on page 179)
2 tablespoons soy sauce or tamari
1 teaspoon chili powder
1 teaspoon ground coriander
½ teaspoon ground cumin
½ teaspoon dried basil
¼ teaspoon dried thyme
Pinch of cayenne pepper
1 cup grated cheese of your choice, optional

Cook the bulgur as directed in Cooking Grains (page 178).

Heat the oil in a large skillet. When it is hot, add the broccoli, onion, and garlic. Sauté over moderately low heat until the broccoli is tender-crisp, stirring frequently. Add the tomatoes, then all the remaining ingredients including the cooked beans and bulgur. Mix together and cook over low heat, stirring occasionally, for 10 minutes.

4 to 6 servings.

> **"Ceres, most bounteous lady, thy rich leas of Wheat, Rye, Barley, Vetches, Oats, and Pease."**
>
> —William Shakespeare
> *The Tempest* (ca. 1611)

KASHA VARNITCHKES

The Jewish classic of buckwheat groats and egg noodles is updated here, lightly herbed and flavored with soy sauce. Peas are added for bright color.

1 cup buckwheat groats (kasha)
1 egg (for cooking groats)
3 tablespoons butter
1 medium onion, chopped
2 medium celery stalks, chopped
¼ pound (115 g) fine egg noodles
1 cup steamed fresh or (thawed) frozen green peas
½ teaspoon paprika
½ teaspoon dried dill
¼ teaspoon dried marjoram
Pinch of dried thyme
Freshly ground pepper to taste
Soy sauce or tamari to taste

Cook the buckwheat groats as directed in Cooking Grains (page 178), using a large skillet.

In the meantime, heat 2 tablespoons of the butter in a small skillet until it foams. Add the onion and celery and sauté over moderately low heat until they are lightly browned.

In the last 10 minutes or so of cooking the groats, begin cooking the egg noodles *al dente*, and drain them when done. (Watch them carefully—they cook very quickly.)

When the groats are done, add to them the sautéed onion and celery, the cooked noodles, the remaining tablespoon of butter, and the rest of the ingredients. Toss together and continue to cook just until everything is thoroughly heated through. If the mixture seems a little dry, add just enough water to make it moist.

4 to 6 servings.

> **"The Goddess ov korn iz also the Goddess ov oats, and barley, and bukwheat. Her name is Series, she is a mithological woman, and like menny wimmen now a daze, she is hard tew lokate."**
>
> —Josh Billings
> *His Works, Complete* (1876)

Rice cultivation probably originated in Eastern Asia and, as has already been mentioned, is the staff of life for half the human race. Rice has always been so highly regarded by the Chinese they have traditionally said "Have you eaten your rice today?" in the same way that we would say "How do you do?" According to Sir James Frazer, author of The Golden Bough, other cultures, particularly the Indonesians, believed that rice contained a soul, and treated the rice in bloom with the same deference with which they may have treated a pregnant woman. Loud noises were not allowed in the rice field lest the rice-souls be frightened, and the growing rice would be fed the same foods that might be given an expectant mother.

RICE SKILLET PIE WITH NUTS AND SPROUTS

This is a very good way to use up leftover rice.

3 eggs, lightly beaten
2/3 cup raw (about 1 1/2 cups cooked) brown rice, prepared following the directions on page 178
1/3 cup finely chopped walnuts
1/2 cup firmly packed alfalfa sprouts, separated with a fork
1 cup firmly packed grated Cheddar cheese
1/4 cup wheat germ
1/4 cup finely chopped celery
2 tablespoons minced chives
3 tablespoons soy sauce or tamari, more or less to taste
1/2 teaspoon paprika
1/2 teaspoon ground cumin
Pinch of cayenne pepper

In a mixing bowl, combine the lightly beaten eggs with the rice and all the remaining ingredients and mix thoroughly. Prepare as directed in "How to Fry and Flip a Skillet Pie or Frittata" (page 180).

4 to 6 servings.

TANGY BAKED RICE
WITH STRING BEANS

Lemon and sour cream combine to give this casserole a zesty flavor.

2 tablespoons butter
1 medium onion, chopped
1 clove garlic, minced
1 cup sliced mushrooms
**3/4 cup raw brown rice, cooked following
    the directions on page 178**
**3 cups string beans, cut into 1-inch (2 1/2
    cm) pieces and steamed**
**1 cup firmly packed grated mild
    white cheese**
3/4 cup sour cream
Juice of 1 lemon
1 teaspoon dried dill
1 teaspoon dried summer savory
1/4 teaspoon dried thyme
1/4 teaspoon dried marjoram
**Salt and freshly ground black pepper
    to taste**
Wheat germ for topping

Preheat the oven to 375°F (190°C). Heat the butter in a skillet until it foams. Add the onion and garlic and sauté until the onion is translucent. Add the mushrooms and sauté until the onion is golden.

Combine the rice with the string beans and the sautéed vegetables in a large mixing bowl. Add the remaining ingredients and mix thoroughly. Pour into an oiled, 9- by 9-inch (23 by 23 cm) casserole dish, sprinkle with wheat germ. Bake for 25 to 30 minutes.

4 to 6 servings.

SAFFRON FRUITED RICE

In sixteenth-century England, if one was in especially good spirits, they were jestingly said to have slept in a bag of saffron, as it was considered a highly exhilarating spice. Its color is gorgeous, but unfortunately, saffron is extremely expensive. For similar effect, substitute turmeric to color this exotic fruited rice.

2 tablespoons butter
1 medium onion, chopped
**1 large sweet apple, peeled, cored,
    and diced**
**1 1/3 cups raw brown rice, cooked following
    the directions on page 178**
1/3 cup chopped nuts of your choice
1/3 cup raisins or currants
**1/3 cup chopped dried fruit (apricots,
    dates, or black figs, or a combination)**
2 to 3 tablespoons honey, to taste
3 tablespoons soy sauce or tamari
2 tablespoons wheat germ
1 1/4 teaspoons powdered saffron
1/4 teaspoon cinnamon
1/4 teaspoon nutmeg
1/2 cup plain yogurt

Heat the butter in a large skillet. When it begins to foam, add the onion and sauté over moderately low heat until it is translucent. Add the apple and sauté until it softens, about 3 or 4 minutes.

Add the remaining ingredients, except the yogurt, and cook over low heat, stirring frequently, for 10 to 12 minutes. Stir in the yogurt and serve.

4 to 6 servings.

THE HOPEFUL SIGN

An inn-sign, through orchards half-discerned,
Promises shelter and drink well earned.
Through water-weeds the pond's geese make
their way;
Midst elms and mulberry trees the swallows play.
The garden's chives are ready to repair;
The scent of young rice perfumes all the air.
When want is banished, as in times like these,
The spinner and the ploughman take their ease.

—Chinese poem
from the Hung-lou Meng

BROCCOLI AND PARSLEY RICE

3 tablespoons butter
3 cups finely chopped broccoli
1 medium onion, finely chopped
1 large celery stalk, chopped
1/2 cup chopped fresh parsley
**1 1/3 cups raw brown rice, cooked following
the directions on page 178**
2 cups grated sharp Cheddar cheese
1 cup light cream
1 teaspoon dried dill
1 teaspoon dried marjoram
1/2 teaspoon dried summer savory
Salt and freshly ground pepper to taste
Wheat germ or sesame seeds for topping

Preheat the oven to 375°F (190°C).

Heat the butter in a large skillet until it foams. Add the broccoli, onion, and celery, and sauté over moderately low heat until all are tender and the onion is just beginning to brown. Add the parsley and sauté just until it is slightly wilted.

In a mixing bowl, combine the cooked rice with the vegetable mixture and all the remaining ingredients. Mix thoroughly and pour into an oiled, large shallow baking dish. Pat the mixture in smoothly and sprinkle the wheat germ or sesame seeds over the top.

Bake for 35 to 40 minutes, or until the top is nicely browned.

6 servings.

PEANUT RICE AND TOFU

If you plan on having leftovers from this dish, add only part of the peanuts to the portion of the dish you will be using immediately, and save the remaining peanuts to add when you reheat the rest. Otherwise, they will absorb moisture and lose the texture and flavor which give this dish such a nice crunch.

2 tablespoons sesame oil
1 medium green pepper, diced
4 bunches scallions, chopped
2 cloves garlic, minced
**3 tablespoons soy sauce or tamari, or
more to taste**
1 tablespoon honey
**1 teaspoon freshly grated ginger, more or
less to taste**
**1 1/3 cups raw brown rice, cooked following
the directions on page 178**
1/2 cup peanut halves
2 cakes tofu (bean curd), diced

Heat the sesame oil in a large skillet. When it is hot, add the green pepper, scallions, and garlic, and sauté over moderate heat until the green pepper is tender. Add the soy sauce, honey, and ginger and stir well.

Add the cooked rice and mix together thoroughly. Taste to determine if you'd like to add a little more soy sauce or perhaps another drop or two of sesame oil. Cook on very low heat for 7 to 8 minutes, stirring frequently.

Stir in the peanuts and tofu and cook just until everything is well heated through.

4 to 6 servings.

> **"She who is the wife of one man cannot eat the rice of two."**
>
> —Chinese Proverb

BARLEY AND MUSHROOM PILAF

1 cup raw barley
2 tablespoons safflower or vegetable oil
1 medium onion, chopped
2 medium celery stalks, chopped
2 cloves garlic, minced
2 cups coarsely chopped mushrooms
3 tablespoons finely chopped fresh parsley
1¼ cups cooked or canned navy or great northern beans (about ½ cup raw, cooked following the directions on page 179)
½ cup plain yogurt
3 tablespoons soy sauce or tamari
1 tablespoon honey
½ teaspoon dried dill
½ teaspoon dried basil
¼ teaspoon dried marjoram
Freshly ground pepper to taste

Cook the barley as directed in Cooking Grains (page 178).

Heat the oil in a large skillet. When it is hot, add the onion, celery and garlic. Sauté over moderately low heat until the onion is translucent. Add the mushrooms and parsley and sauté until the vegetables are just tender.

Add the beans, barley, and the remaining ingredients to the skillet and cook, stirring frequently, until thoroughly heated through.

6 servings.

Barley is one of the most ancient of cultivated grains. Traditionally the symbol of abundance in India, barley was associated with birth and wedding rituals, and the god Indra was referred to as "he who ripens barley."

MILLET STUFFED PEPPERS

Millet is a tiny, round yellow cereal grain that is not often used in this country but is a staple in other cultures. It cooks to an almost mush texture, tastes bland but pleasant, and makes a nice alternative to rice as a bed of grains, or like here, for stuffing vegetables.

2/3 cup raw millet
4 large green peppers
2 tablespoons butter
1 large onion, chopped
1 clove garlic, minced
2 tablespoons wheat germ
3/4 cup grated mild cheese of your choice
1/3 cup plain yogurt
1 teaspoon dried marjoram or summer savory
Salt and freshly ground pepper to taste
Extra wheat germ for topping
Extra grated cheese for topping
Paprika for garnish

Cook the millet as directed in Cooking Grains (page 178). Preheat the oven to 325°F (165°C).

Bring a large pot of water to a boil. Cut each pepper in half and remove seeds, membranes, and stem ends. When the water is boiling rapidly, drop the peppers in and cook at a slow boil for 3 minutes. Drain immediately and when cool enough to handle, arrange on a lightly oiled baking dish. Salt lightly if desired.

Heat the butter in a large skillet. When it foams, add the onion and garlic and sauté over moderately low heat until the onion is golden. Add the millet, wheat germ, cheese, yogurt, and seasonings and stir together.

Stuff each pepper half generously with the millet mixture. Top with extra wheat germ and grated cheese, and sprinkle each one with a little paprika for color.

Bake for 30 to 35 minutes, or until the peppers are done to your liking.

4 generous servings.

"One grain fills not the sack, but helps his fellows."

—George Herbert
Jacula Prudentum (1640)

COUSCOUS STUFFED EGGPLANT

Couscous is presteamed, cracked semolina and is the lightest and fluffiest of all grains. It makes an excellent bed of grains for many types of dishes; it is also ideal as a stuffing, as it quickly absorbs all the flavors around it.

1 cup raw couscous
2 medium eggplants
3 tablespoons olive oil
3 to 4 cloves garlic, minced
5 bunches scallions, chopped
3 medium ripe tomatoes, chopped
4 tablespoons wheat germ
2 tablespoons lemon juice
1/4 cup minced fresh parsley or basil
1 teaspoon ground cumin
1 teaspoon chili powder
1/2 teaspoon ground turmeric, optional
Salt and freshly ground pepper to taste
1 cup plain yogurt

Prepare the couscous as directed in Cooking Grains (page 178). Preheat the oven to 375°F (190°C).

Cut the stem ends off the eggplants and cut each in half lengthwise. With a sharp knife, carefully cut away the eggplant pulp, leaving a shell about 1/2-inch (1½ cm) wide all around. Chop the eggplant pulp that you have removed into small dice. Heat the olive oil and 2 tablespoons of water in a large skillet. When hot, add the diced eggplant and garlic, and, covered, cook over low heat until the eggplant is tender but still firm. Stir occasionally. Add the scallions and tomatoes and cook just until they have softened a bit. Add the remaining ingredients, including the couscous, stir together, and remove from the heat.

Arrange the eggplant shells in a lightly oiled, shallow baking dish. Stuff with the couscous mixture and bake for 35 to 40 minutes, or until the eggplant shell is easily pierced through with a fork, but has not collapsed.

4 servings.

Corn was probably first cultivated by the ancient Aztecs, Mayas, and other Indians of that period. To them, corn was the staff of life, just as rice has always been in the Orient, and was held in the same reverence. They developed many colorful varieties of corn (also known as maize), and with this cultivation grew elaborate ceremonies, rituals, and legends, along with various corn gods, goddesses and spirits.

One South American legend tells of two brothers who took shelter on a mountaintop after a flood. There was no food anywhere. The brothers were nearly starved when suddenly two parrots appeared and offered them corn. Each day after that, the same parrots brought corn with which the brothers fed themselves. One day, one of the men caught one of the parrots. The parrot turned into a lovely maiden and she set about to teach the brothers how to cultivate corn.

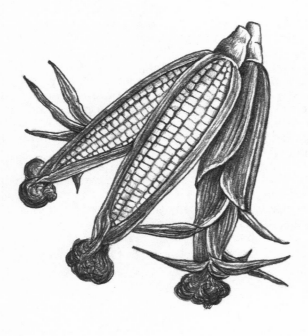

CORN ENCHILADAS

1 cup cooked or canned red or kidney beans (about ⅓ to ½ cup raw, cooked following the directions on page 179)
2 tablespoons olive oil
1 medium onion, chopped
1 14-ounce (400g) can imported plum tomatoes, lightly drained and chopped
1½ cups cooked fresh or (thawed) frozen corn kernels
1 teaspoon chili powder, or more to taste
1 teaspoon dried oregano
½ teaspoon ground cumin
½ teaspoon ground coriander
¼ teaspoon dry mustard
1 tablespoon soy sauce or tamari
2 medium ripe tomatoes, grated
1 small onion, grated
Salt and freshly ground pepper to taste
1 tablespoon minced cilantro or parsley
8 soft corn tortillas
1½ cups grated Cheddar or Monterey Jack cheese

Preheat the oven to 350°F (180°C).

Mash the cooked or canned beans well. Heat the oil in a large skillet. When it is hot, add the onion and sauté over moderately low heat until it is translucent. Add the beans, canned tomatoes, corn, and seasonings. Stir together and cook over moderately low heat for 10 minutes, stirring occasionally.

Cut the fresh tomatoes in half and grate them down to the skin. Combine them with the grated onion, salt, pepper and cilantro or parsley. Set aside.

If the tortillas seem stiff, heat a large, dry skillet and heat each one on both sides for a few seconds, just until they become flexible.

Lightly oil one or two shallow baking dishes. Spoon a bit of the corn and bean mixture down the middle of each tortilla, fold one side over the other, and arrange on the baking dishes.

Spoon the fresh tomato mixture over them evenly, and top with the grated cheese. Bake for 20 to 25 minutes, or until the cheese is bubbly.

4 servings.

COLORFUL CORN CASSEROLE

2 tablespoons butter
1 medium onion, chopped
1 medium sweet red or green pepper, chopped
3 eggs, beaten
3 cups cooked fresh or (thawed) frozen corn kernels
1 cup grated zucchini
1/3 cup cornmeal
1/3 cup chopped green olives
1 8-ounce (225g) can whole tomatoes with liquid, chopped
1 1/2 cups grated sharp Cheddar cheese
1/2 teaspoon chili powder
1/2 teaspoon ground coriander
1/4 teaspoon ground turmeric, optional
1/2 teaspoon Dijon mustard
Salt and freshly ground pepper to taste

Preheat the oven to 350°F (180°C).

Heat the butter in a skillet until it foams. Add the onion and sauté over moderately low heat until it is translucent. Add the red or green pepper and sauté until both are lightly browned.

In a mixing bowl, combine the beaten eggs with the sautéed vegetables and the remaining ingredients. Mix thoroughly, and pour into an oiled, large shallow baking dish. Bake for 30 to 35 minutes.

4 to 6 servings.

It is no longer common knowledge that beans were formerly forbidden foods, held under the most solemn taboos. Among the ancient Egyptians, beans were sacred, and were actually worshipped. They were associated with the doctrines of immortality and transmigration, and eating them was forbidden due to the belief that they possessed a soul. In ancient Greece, eating beans was forbidden not because they were objects of worship, but of scorn. They were considered evil, a negative influence on dreams, and were associated with lunacy. Oddly, beans were held in greatest contempt by Pythagoras, the father of Western vegetarianism. Pythagoras would be duly ashamed if he knew that he was depriving his considerable legion of followers of a protein-rich vegetarian staple.

"The Pythagoreans make a point of prohibiting the use of beans, as if thereby the soul and not the belly was filled with wind!"

—Cicero
De Divination (44 B.C.)

OPEN-FACED AVOCADO BEAN TACOS

4 cups cooked or canned beans (about 1½ to 1⅔ cups raw—any red or white bean is fine, cooked following the directions on page 179)
8 soft corn tortillas
2 tablespoons olive oil
1 medium green pepper, finely chopped
1 medium onion, finely chopped
2 cloves garlic, minced
2 tablespoons soy sauce or tamari
2 teaspoons chili powder, more or less to taste
1 teaspoon ground coriander
1 teaspoon ground cumin
½ teaspoon dry mustard
Cayenne pepper or hot sauce to taste, optional
2 cups tomato sauce
1 large ripe avocado, finely diced
1 large ripe tomato, finely chopped
Shredded lettuce or alfalfa sprouts
Grated Cheddar cheese, sour cream, or plain yogurt

Mash the cooked or canned beans or purée them well. Heat a dry skillet until it is very hot. Toast each tortilla over moderate heat, on both sides until crisp.

Heat the olive oil in a large skillet. When hot, add the green pepper, onion, and garlic and sauté over moderately low heat until all are tender but not browned. Add the beans, seasonings, and tomato sauce and stir well. Cook over low heat for 10 minutes, stirring occasionally.

In the meantime, prepare the raw vegetables, and the cheese if you're using it. Assemble the tacos as follows: A generous bed of lettuce or alfalfa sprouts on the tortilla, followed by the bean mixture, then some diced avocado and tomato, topped with a little bit of grated cheese, sour cream, or yogurt. To eat, pick the whole thing up, or break it in half and pick it up, or cut small pieces off with a knife and fork.

Makes 8 tacos—between 4 and 8 servings, depending on appetites and how much other food you're serving.

KIDNEY BEAN AND VEGETABLE CHILI

For those just getting acquainted with making or eating entrées composed of beans and grains, this saucy chili is almost invariably a favorite.

2 tablespoons olive oil
1 large onion, chopped
1 medium green pepper, chopped
1 small zucchini, thinly sliced
1 cup cooked fresh or (thawed) frozen corn kernels
1 14-ounce (400g) can imported plum tomatoes with liquid, chopped
1 6-ounce (180g) can tomato paste
3 tablespoons soy sauce or tamari
2 teaspoons chili powder, more or less to taste
1 teaspoon ground cumin
1/2 teaspoon ground coriander
1/2 teaspoon dried oregano
1/4 teaspoon dried thyme
Cayenne pepper to taste, optional
2 1/2 cups cooked or canned kidney beans (about 1 cup raw, cooked following the directions on page 179)
Pickled green chilies for garnish, optional
Cheddar cheese wedges for garnish, optional

Heat the oil in a very large skillet. When it is hot, add the onion and sauté over moderately low heat until the onion is translucent. Add the green pepper and sauté until it softens somewhat. Add the remaining ingredients, including the beans, and simmer over very low heat for 15 minutes, stirring occasionally. Serve on its own in bowls garnished with a green chili and wedge of Cheddar cheese, or, even better, over brown rice.

4 to 6 servings.

Did you ever wonder why beans have seams? In Grimm's Fairy Tales, a bean laughs so hard at the demise of her friends the Straw and the Coal, that her sides split. A kind tailor passing by spotted her and sewed her sides back together. Ever since, beans have had seams.

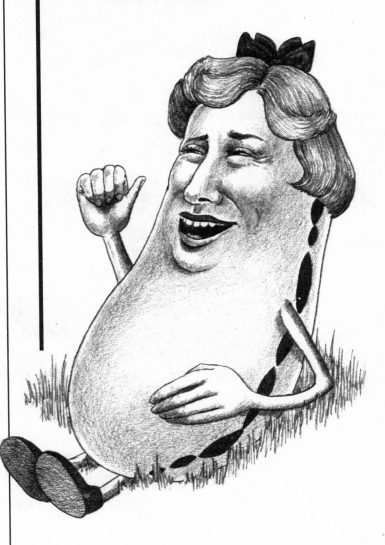

In the early Greek and Roman eras, beans were widely used as ballots. Casting a white bean signified an affirmative vote, whereas a dark bean was a negative vote. Previously, it was mentioned that beans have had to overcome their supernatural taboos, but by the Christian era, abstention from beans took on political overtones. Plutarch, circa 95 A.D., claimed that to "abstain from beans" meant that one should stay out of politics. Others after him also wrote of beans in this manner.

THREE BEANS AND TWO CHEESES

Instead of forbidding beans or voting with them, the ancients would have done well to enjoy them in savory baked casseroles such as those on this page.

1 heaping cup cooked or canned red or kidney beans (about 1/3 to 1/2 cup raw)
1 heaping cup cooked or canned navy or great northern beans (about 1/3 to 1/2 cup raw)
2 cups cooked or canned chick-peas (about 3/4 cup raw)
1 tablespoon safflower or vegetable oil
1 medium onion, chopped
1 small green pepper, chopped
1 14-ounce (400g) can imported plum tomatoes with liquid, chopped
3 tablespoons soy sauce or tamari
2 tablespoons honey
1 teaspoon chili powder, or more to taste
1 teaspoon ground coriander
1 teaspoon paprika
1 teaspoon dried summer savory
1 teaspoon dried oregano
1/2 teaspoon dry mustard
1 cup firmly packed grated Cheddar cheese
1 cup firmly packed grated Monterey Jack cheese

Cook the beans following the directions on page 179. Preheat the oven to 400°F (205°C).

Combine the cooked beans in a mixing bowl and set aside. Heat the oil in a small skillet. When hot, add the onion and sauté until it is translucent. Add the green pepper and sauté until both are lightly browned, then add them to the beans along with the remaining ingredients, except the cheeses. Mix thoroughly. Lightly oil a large, shallow baking casserole and pour the bean mixture into it. Top with the grated cheeses. Bake for 25 minutes. Serve over grains; I particularly recommend couscous, as its lightness is a nice complement to the heartiness of the beans.

4 to 6 servings.

BOSTON BAKED BEANS

Traditionally, the beans in this dish were oven-cooked for 5 to 8 hours. By precooking the beans, the baking time is cut down considerably. Cook the beans to the texture you like, since the additional baking doesn't seem to soften them any further.

4 cups cooked or canned navy beans (about 1 2/3 cups raw, cooked following the directions on page 179)
1 6-ounce (180g) can tomato paste
1/3 cup molasses
2 tablespoons brown sugar
1 teaspoon paprika
1/2 teaspoon dry mustard
Pinch of cayenne pepper
2 to 3 tablespoons soy sauce or tamari
1 tablespoon safflower or vegetable oil
1 large onion, sliced into rings

Preheat the oven to 350°F (180°C).

Combine all the ingredients, except the oil and onion in a mixing bowl. Mix thoroughly and pour into 9-by 9-inch (23 by 23 cm) baking casserole. Cover and bake 30 minutes.

Heat the oil in a skillet. When it is hot, add the onion, stirring to separate the rings, and sauté until brown. After the beans have baked for 30 minutes, top with the onions and bake, uncovered, for another 10 minutes.

Serve on its own or over rice. This tastes good eaten with a wedge of sharp Cheddar cheese.

6 servings.

"To absteine from beanes, that is not to meddle in civile affaires...for in the old times the election of magistrates was made by the pullyng of beanes."

—John Lyly
Euphues (1579)

CHICK-PEA CROQUETTES

These nicely spiced croquettes can be served as a protein supplement to grains or vegetables, and are also good stuffed in warm pita bread, along with shredded lettuce, tomatoes, and Tofu "Mayonnaise" or one of its variations (page 52).

1 tablespoon olive oil
1 small green pepper, finely chopped
1 clove garlic, minced
2 cups cooked or canned chick-peas
    (about ³/₄ cup raw, cooked following
    the directions on page 179)
2 hard-boiled eggs
2 eggs, beaten
¹/₄ cup finely chopped black or green olives
3 tablespoons plain yogurt
¹/₄ cup cornmeal
¹/₄ cup wheat germ
1 teaspoon ground cumin
¹/₂ teaspoon dried thyme
¹/₂ teaspoon dried basil
¹/₄ teaspoon ground coriander
¹/₄ teaspoon dried sage
¹/₄ teaspoon dry mustard
Salt and freshly ground pepper to taste
Oil for frying

Heat the olive oil in a small skillet. When it is hot, add the green pepper and garlic and sauté over moderately low heat until the green pepper is tender but not browned.

In a large mixing bowl, mash the chick-peas and the hard-boiled eggs together as finely as you can. Add the beaten eggs and all the remaining ingredients and mix together thoroughly. Cover and refrigerate for 30 minutes to 1 hour.

Heat enough oil to coat the bottom of a large skillet. When it is very hot, turn the heat to moderate. Shape the chick-pea mixture into palm-shaped croquettes and fry them on both sides until nicely browned. Use more oil as needed. Drain the croquettes on paper towels.

Makes about 12 croquettes.

CHICK-PEAS IN OLIVE-TAHINI SAUCE

As Middle Eastern cooks have known for a long time, the flavors of chick-peas and tahini (sesame paste) are exceptionally compatible. This is an offbeat but very interesting way to combine them.

2 tablespoons olive oil
2 cloves garlic, minced
1 small onion, finely chopped
3 large celery stalks, chopped
1 medium sweet red or green pepper,
    finely chopped
1 recipe Olive-Tahini Sauce (page 51)
3 heaping cups cooked or canned
    chick-peas (about 1¹/₄ cups raw,
    cooked following the directions on
    page 179)
¹/₄ cup wheat germ
1 tablespoon soy sauce or tamari, optional
¹/₂ teaspoon dried marjoram
¹/₄ teaspoon ground coriander
Freshly ground pepper to taste

Heat the oil in a large skillet. When it is hot, add the garlic, onion, and celery and sauté over moderately low heat until the onion is translucent. Add the sweet pepper and sauté until the vegetables are lightly browned. Remove from the heat and pour the Olive-Tahini sauce into the skillet along with the remaining ingredients. Return to low heat and simmer for 5 to 7 minutes. Serve on its own or over grains.

4 to 6 servings.

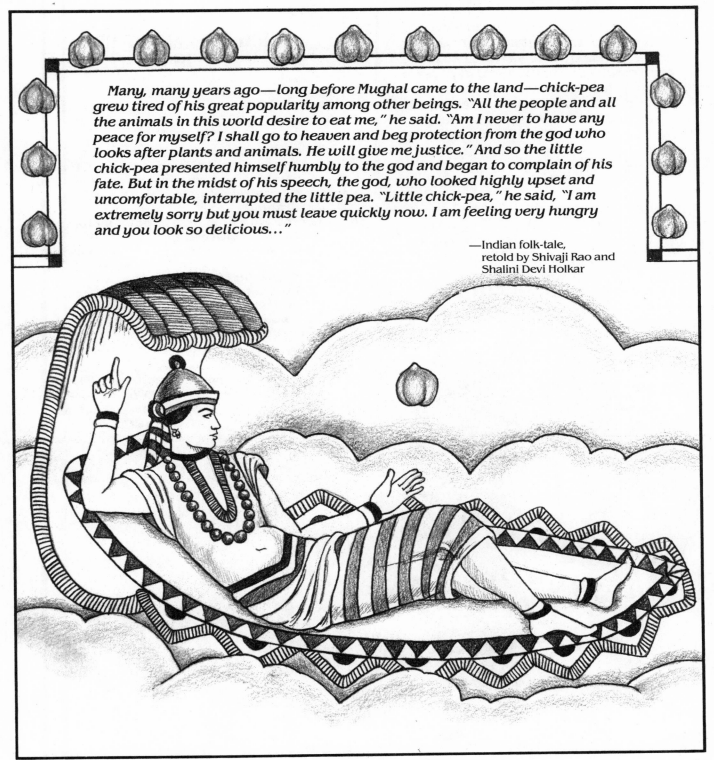

Many, many years ago—long before Mughal came to the land—chick-pea grew tired of his great popularity among other beings. "All the people and all the animals in this world desire to eat me," he said. "Am I never to have any peace for myself? I shall go to heaven and beg protection from the god who looks after plants and animals. He will give me justice." And so the little chick-pea presented himself humbly to the god and began to complain of his fate. But in the midst of his speech, the god, who looked highly upset and uncomfortable, interrupted the little pea. "Little chick-pea," he said, "I am extremely sorry but you must leave quickly now. I am feeling very hungry and you look so delicious..."

—Indian folk-tale,
retold by Shivaji Rao and
Shalini Devi Holkar

Lentils have been cultivated for thousands of years. They have always been an inexpensive item and have had to overcome a certain snobbery as a "poor man's" food. These little legumes are packed with protein and have become a vegetarian staple. Prepared carefully, they can be as enticing as a more exotic food.

Your Terrine de Lentils, Madame

CURRIED LENTILS WITH SPINACH

Lentils have a definite affinity with curry spices, which, combined with the tomatoes here form a rich, savory broth.

1 cup raw lentils
1 tablespoon olive oil
2 cloves garlic, minced
½ pound (225g) spinach leaves, preferably fresh, stemmed, washed, and chopped, or equivalent of frozen, thawed and drained
1 14-ounce (400g) can imported plum tomatoes with liquid, chopped
2 to 3 tablespoons soy sauce or tamari
2 teaspoons good curry powder or Home-Mixed Curry (page 170), more or less to taste
¼ teaspoon freshly grated ginger
¼ teaspoon cinnamon
¼ teaspoon nutmeg

Wash and sort the lentils and cook until they are tender but firm (see Cooking Beans, page 179).

Heat the olive oil in a large skillet. When it is hot, add the garlic and sauté over moderately low heat for 1 minute or so. Add the spinach leaves, cover, and steam until they are wilted.

Add the lentils and the remaining ingredients to the skillet. Cover and simmer over very low heat for 15 minutes. Serve over grains. This is especially good over brown rice or couscous; or, for a delicious change of pace, try this over mashed potatoes.

4 to 6 servings.

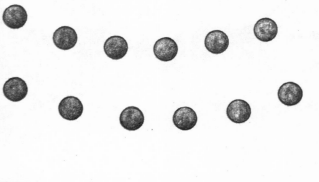

SWEET AND SOUR LENTILS WITH FINE NOODLES

1 cup raw lentils
¼ cup (scant) soy sauce or tamari
¼ cup honey
⅓ cup rice vinegar or white vinegar
¾ teaspoon freshly grated ginger
1 heaping cup raw fine egg noodles
2 tablespoons sesame oil
1 clove garlic, minced
1 large carrot, thinly sliced
½ medium green pepper, finely chopped
4 to 5 bunches scallions, chopped

Wash and sort the lentils and cook until they are tender but still firm (see Cooking Beans, page 179).

In a small bowl, combine the soy sauce, honey, vinegar, and ginger, and mix well. Set aside.

Cook the egg noodles *al dente*, drain and set them aside. (Watch them carefully—they cook very quickly.)

Heat the sesame oil in a large skillet. When it is hot, add the garlic and carrot and sauté over moderately low heat until the carrot is tender-crisp. Add the green pepper and scallions and sauté just until the scallions wilt a bit. Add the cooked lentils and the sweet and sour mixture; simmer over low heat for 10 minutes, then add the noodles and simmer just until they are heated through.

4 to 6 servings.

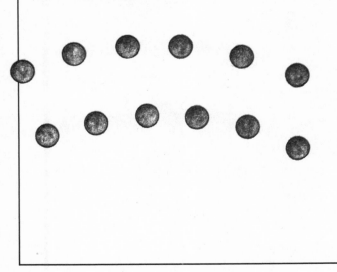

CHILI LENTIL AND RICE PILAF

This is a good, basic "everyday" dish, substantial and high in protein, and it keeps very well for several days. A nice big salad is enough to complete the meal.

1 cup raw lentils
1 cup raw brown rice
2 cloves garlic, minced
2 bay leaves
2 tablespoons soy sauce or tamari
2 tablespoons olive oil
1 large onion, chopped
1½ to 2 cups steamed green vegetables, such as chopped broccoli or string beans, cut into 1-inch (2½ cm) pieces, or a combination
1 14-ounce (400g) can imported plum tomatoes with liquid, chopped
1 6-ounce (180g) can tomato paste
2 teaspoons chili powder, more or less to taste
1 teaspoon ground cumin
1 teaspoon dried summer savory
1 teaspoon paprika
½ teaspoon dried oregano
¼ teaspoon dry mustard
Pinch of cayenne pepper
Extra soy sauce or tamari to taste

Place the lentils and rice, after washing them, in a large pot along with the garlic, bay leaves, and soy sauce. Add 5 cups of water and bring to a boil. Cover and simmer over low heat. Check after about 25 minutes, stir, and continue to simmer, uncovered, until done. Drain off any excess liquid.

Heat the oil in a large skillet. When it is hot, add the onion and sauté over moderately low heat until golden. Add the lentils and rice and all the remaining ingredients, stir well and simmer over low heat for 8 to 10 minutes.

Serves 6.

Variation: Although it is not necessary for protein content, this tastes very good with a little Cheddar cheese sprinkled over the top of each serving.

> **"***Green Peas, boiled carefully with onions, and powdered with cinnamon, ginger, and cardamoms, well pounded, create for the consumer considerable amorous passion and strength in coitus.* **"**

—Shaykh Nefzawi
The Perfumed Garden (ca. 1400)

LUSTY CURRIED PEAS

Find out for yourself whether this spicy treat really does ignite the passions.

2 medium sweet potatoes
4 cups steamed fresh or (thawed) frozen green peas
2 tablespoons butter
1 large onion, chopped
1 14-ounce (400g) can imported plum tomatoes with liquid, chopped
1 tablespoon honey
1 teaspoon cinnamon
1 teaspoon ground cumin
½ teaspoon ground turmeric
½ teaspoon freshly grated ginger
½ teaspoon ground cardamom, or the seeds from 3 to 4 cardamom pods
¼ teaspoon dry mustard
Salt to taste
Cayenne pepper to taste, optional
Plain yogurt

Cook or bake the potatoes until tender but still firm. When cool enough to handle, peel and dice them. Have ready the peas, either steamed as you like them, or thawed if you're using frozen.

Heat the butter in a large skillet until it is foamy. Add the onion and sauté until it is translucent. Add the potatoes, peas, the tomatoes, ¼ cup of water and the remaining ingredients, except the yogurt. Stir together and simmer over very low heat for 10 to 12 minutes. Serve the yogurt separately, so a spoonful or two can be stirred into each serving.

4 to 6 servings.

RICE AND PEAS WITH CURRY-CHEESE SAUCE

Perhaps this mild curry would have tempted Beau Brummell to give peas another try.

1 1/3 cups raw brown rice
2 tablespoons soy sauce or tamari
2 tablespoons butter
2 to 3 cloves garlic, minced
1 large celery stalk, finely chopped
**1/4 cup finely chopped cilantro or fresh
    parsley**
1 recipe Curry-Cheese Sauce (page 49)
**2 cups steamed fresh or (thawed) frozen
    green peas**
2 teaspoons dried mint
1/4 teaspoon nutmeg
**1/4 teaspoon ground cumin, or more to
    taste**
1/4 teaspoon ground turmeric, optional
Additional soy sauce or tamari to taste
1/2 cup plain yogurt
**Sesame seeds or chopped peanuts for
    garnish**

Cook the rice as directed in Cooking Grains (page 178), adding the soy sauce or tamari to the cooking water. When it is done, transfer to a casserole dish and cover tightly.

Heat the butter in a large skillet. When it foams, add the garlic and celery and sauté over moderately low heat. Just before the vegetables brown, add the cilantro, and sauté until the celery is lightly browned. Remove from the heat and cover.

Pour the Curry Cheese Sauce over the celery and herb mixture in the skillet and add the peas and seasonings. Return to low heat until the sauce is bubbly. Pour the mixture over the rice, add the yogurt, and mix thoroughly.

Garnish each serving with sesame seeds or chopped peanuts.

6 servings.

George Bryan Brummell (1778–1840), better known as Beau Brummell, was the undisputed fashion leader of early nineteenth-century England. Also known as something of a wit, when asked if he never ate vegetables, replied,

"I once ate a pea."

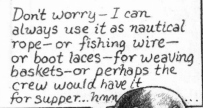

Don't worry — I can always use it as nautical rope — or fishing wire — or boot laces — for weaving baskets — or perhaps the crew would have it for supper...hmm......

PASTA

A romantic legend tells of how spaghetti first arrived in Italy. In the thirteenth century, Marco Polo voyaged to China, and during his stay, he became enamored of a lovely Chinese maiden. One sunny day, he and his beloved became engrossed with one another while she was preparing her daily batch of bread dough. The maiden neglected to see that the dough was overflowing, dripping in long, thin strings. Soon, the hot sun dried it up. To hide his sweetheart's mistake, Marco Polo gathered up the dough strings and took them back to his ship, where the cook boiled them in a broth that night. The dish was an immediate hit with the crew, and upon the ship's return to Italy, the sailors spread the word of this new delicacy, where it soon became a favorite. Take this charming legend as you might eat your spaghetti—with a grain of salt.

Pasta, in various forms called macaroni or noodles, has had its origins traced as far back as China of 5000 B.C. A versatile, nutritious vehicle for tasty sauces and vegetables in numerous combinations, it is one of those foods that nearly everyone loves. The usual pastas are made of semolina, which is the heart of durum wheat, and the great variety of shapes and sizes are fun to experiment with. Whole wheat pastas come in many varieties, too. Try these for a change of pace.

Until fairly recently, pasta was more often referred to as macaroni, which is most commonly taken to mean the tubular variety, and that is the name under which it entered England in the eighteenth century. More on that later in this chapter. There are two interesting versions as to how macaroni got its name. In one legend, a thirteenth-century king who was something of an epicure was served this new type of dish consisting of delicious tubes covered with a rich sauce. Upon tasting it, he exclaimed, "Ma Caroni!" which means something like "how very dear," that is, dear as in darling. The other version has it that German bakers made dough figures in the shape of men, shells, stars, etc. These were taken to Italy by German merchants. The Italians were reluctant to buy them due to their large size and high price and protested "Ma Caroni!"—again "how very dear," but this time interpreted as "how very expensive." The German bakers reduced the size and price of the dough shapes but they were from then on called "macaroni."

BAKED PASTA WITH EGGPLANT

Pasta is presented here with some of the best of its companions—eggplant, herbed tomato sauce, and three cheeses.

2 tablespoons olive oil
1 large eggplant, peeled and diced
1 clove garlic, minced
2 cups raw medium-sized shaped pasta, such as rotelle, ziti, shells, etc.
Oil for sautéing
1 large green pepper, cut into julienne strips
¾ cup sliced or chopped black olives
¼ cup chopped fresh parsley
1 recipe Tomato-Herb Pasta Sauce (page 107), eliminating one of the cans of tomato paste
½ pound (225g) ricotta cheese
½ cup grated Parmesan cheese
Salt and freshly ground pepper to taste
1 to 1½ cups grated mozzarella cheese

Preheat oven to 325°F (165°C). Heat the olive oil and ¼ cup water in a large skillet. When hot, add the eggplant and garlic and cook, covered, over moderately low heat, stirring occasionally, until eggplant is tender. At the same time, begin cooking the pasta *al dente*. When it is done, drain immediately.

Heat a few drops of oil in a small skillet. When it is hot, add the green pepper and sauté over moderate heat just until it has lost its raw quality. Remove from the heat and stir in the olives and parsley.

In a mixing bowl, combine the sauce, eggplant, pasta, ricotta, Parmesan cheese, and salt and pepper. Mix thoroughly.

Oil a large shallow baking dish and layer as follows: All of the pasta and eggplant mixture, topped with the green pepper mixture, sprinkled with the grated cheese. Bake for 30 to 35 minutes.

4 to 6 servings.

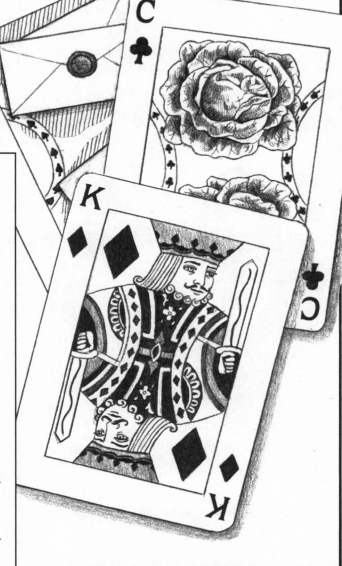

EGG NOODLES WITH RED CABBAGE

The humble cabbage becomes elegant with pasta and cream, and the poppy seeds add a nutty flavor.

1 tablespoon vegetable or safflower oil
4 cups firmly packed, thinly shredded red cabbage
1 medium onion, chopped
½ pound (225g) medium width, flat egg noodles
½ to ¾ cup heavy cream
2 tablespoons butter
2 tablespoons poppy seeds
2 tablespoons wheat germ
½ teaspoon dried dill
⅛ teaspoon dried sage
Salt and freshly ground pepper to taste
½ cup grated Parmesan cheese

Heat the oil and 2 tablespoons of water in a large skillet. When hot, add the cabbage and onion, cover, and cook until tender but not overdone, stirring occasionally. Add more water as needed to keep the mixture moist.

Begin cooking the egg noodles. When cooked *al dente,* drain and place in a large, covered casserole.

When the cabbage is tender, add the cream, butter, and remaining ingredients, except the Parmesan cheese, to the skillet. Simmer over low heat just until well heated through. Pour over the noodles and toss well. Add the Parmesan cheese and toss again.

4 to 6 servings.

'The time has come,' the Walrus said,
'to talk of many things,
Of shoes—and ships—and
sealing wax—
Of Cabbages and Kings...'

—Lewis Carroll
Through the Looking Glass (1871)

"Macaroni"

Yankee Doodle came to town
Riding on a pony
Stuck a feather in his cap
And called it "Macaroni."

These lyrics are familiar to so many English-speaking children, yet who has ever wondered why that feather was called "macaroni"? It's not as nonsensical as it might seem.

SHELLS WITH BEANS AND BROCCOLI

As mentioned in the Vegetables chapter, broccoli is a vegetable of Italian origin, and it has long been known to have a wonderful affinity with pasta. The addition of beans makes this a very substantial dish.

½ **pound (225g) small shell pasta**
2 **tablespoons olive oil**
2 **cloves garlic, minced**
1 **small green pepper, cut into julienne strips**
1 **recipe White Cheese Sauce (page 49)**
2 **cups cooked or canned navy beans (about ¾ cups raw, cooked following the directions on page 179)**
2 **cups broccoli florets, steamed**
½ **cup chopped or sliced black olives**
½ **teaspoon dried basil**
½ **teaspoon dried marjoram**
1 **teaspoon dried oregano**
¼ **teaspoon ground coriander**
Salt and freshly ground pepper to taste
Grated Parmesan cheese for topping

Begin cooking the pasta *al dente.* When it is done, drain and transfer it to a covered casserole dish.

In the meantime, heat the olive oil in a large skillet. When it is hot, add the garlic and sauté over moderately low heat for a minute or so. Add the green pepper and sauté until the pepper is tender but not brown. Remove from the heat.

Pour the White Cheese Sauce into the skillet. Then stir in the beans, broccoli, olives, and seasonings. Return to moderate heat and simmer just until everything is thoroughly heated through. Pour over the pasta in the casserole dish and toss well. Top each serving with grated Parmesan cheese.

6 servings.

PASTA WITH CAULIFLOWER, CURRANTS AND NUTS

Cauliflower is another vegetable that goes beautifully with pasta. The currants give this rich dish an unexpected flavor twist without making it sweet. For a special meal, begin with Mediterranean Broccoli and Mushroom Soup (page 18), then serve this with Eggplant Skillet Pie (page 121) and a green salad.

1½ **cups ricotta cheese**
⅓ **cup grated Parmesan cheese**
½ **cup milk or light cream**
Pinch of nutmeg
½ **pound (225g) medium-sized shaped pasta, such as rotelle, ziti, etc.**
3 **tablespoons olive oil**
1 **small head cauliflower, cut into bite-sized pieces and florets**
1 **egg, beaten**
2 **cloves garlic, minced**
⅓ **cup toasted pine nuts, or** ½ **cup chopped walnuts**
⅓ **cup currants (raisins may be substituted)**
2 **tablespoons butter**
Salt and freshly ground pepper to taste

Combine the first 4 ingredients in a small bowl, mix well and set aside.

Begin cooking the pasta at this point. When it is done, drain it and transfer to a covered casserole dish.

Heat 2 tablespoons of the olive oil in a large skillet. When it is hot, stir-fry the cauliflower pieces over moderate heat until they are tender-crisp. Beat the egg in a bowl large enough to accommodate the cauliflower, then transfer it in and mix until the pieces are evenly coated with the egg.

In the same skillet, heat the remaining olive oil and sauté the garlic over moderately low heat until it is golden. Add the cauliflower and sauté, stirring continuously, until the egg is set. Add the nuts, currants, butter, salt and pepper, and ricotta mixture and simmer just until thoroughly heated through. Pour over the pasta and toss well.

6 servings.

During the 1700s, when an English soldier wrote the lyrics of "Yankee Doodle Dandy," macaroni was new to England and quickly became a very popular, and indeed, quite a fashionable food. As a result, anything elegant or stylish, whether it was clothing, food, music, manners, or a feather in one's cap, was called "macaroni," so positive was the connotation of the word.

Your hat is so simple, yet so smart, and so very, very Macaroni!

LINGUINI AGLIO OLIO WITH ZUCCHINI

A friend who grew up with traditional Italian cookery taught me about Aglio Olio, which means garlic and oil, a very simple but unbelievably delicious and fragrant Italian classic. In the context of this recipe, he offered these thoughts: "In order to cook well, one must use all of one's senses—taste, smell, even feel. When a recipe calls for good olive oil, this doesn't necessarily mean the most expensive one, but one that tastes and smells the best.... Memory serves us well also, as we remember the scents we enjoy...." Aglio Olio produces a scent that is hard to forget. See Easy Corn Frittata (page 67) for a menu suggestion.

1 pound (450g) linguini, broken in half (or substitute thin spaghetti)
½ cup good olive oil (extra-virgin is recommended)
8 cloves garlic, minced
3 medium zucchini, quartered lengthwise and sliced
¼ cup chopped fresh parsley
2 teaspoons dried oregano
Salt and freshly ground pepper to taste
⅔ cup grated Parmesan cheese

Begin cooking the linguini.

Heat half the olive oil in a large skillet. When it is hot, add the garlic and sauté over low heat for 2 minutes, stirring frequently. Add the zucchini and sauté over low heat, stirring frequently. Just before the zucchini is tender, add the parsley and sauté until the parsley is slightly wilted and the zucchini is tender but not browned.

The zucchini and linguini will be done at approximately the same time. When the linguini is *al dente*, drain and immediately transfer it to a large, deep serving casserole. Add the remaining olive oil, the zucchini and garlic mixture, the oregano, and salt and pepper. Toss well. Add the Parmesan cheese and toss again.

Makes 6 generous servings.

"*Garlicke ingendreth naughty and sharp blood.* "

—John Gerarde
The Herball (1636)

CURRIED ZITI WITH BROCCOLI AND CHICK-PEAS

Adding a curried flavor to pasta is not the usual thing to do, but this blend of Italian and Indian flavors works very nicely.

½ pound (225g) ziti
2 tablespoons butter
1 medium onion, chopped
1 to 2 cloves garlic, minced
1 pound very ripe tomatoes, chopped, or 1 14-ounce (400g) can imported plum tomatoes with liquid, chopped
2 tablespoons minced fresh parsley or cilantro
1 recipe Curry Cheese Sauce (page 49)
3 heaping cups broccoli, cut into bite-sized pieces and steamed
1½ cups cooked or canned chick-peas (about ⅔ cup raw, cooked following the directions on page 179)
Salt and freshly ground pepper to taste

Cook the pasta *al dente*. When it is done, drain and transfer it to a large, covered casserole dish.

In the meantime, heat the butter in a large skillet until it foams. Add the onion and garlic and sauté over moderately low heat until golden. If you're using fresh tomatoes, add them and cook until they have softened, then stir in the parsley or cilantro and remove the skillet from heat. If you're using canned tomatoes, simply add them to the skillet along with the parsley and remove from heat.

Add the Curry Cheese Sauce to the skillet. Then add the broccoli, chick-peas, salt and pepper. Return to low heat and simmer for 10 to 15 minutes. Add more curry powder or Home-Mixed Curry if desired.

Pour over the pasta and toss together.
6 servings.

DOUBLE SPINACH NOODLES

½ pound (225g) spinach noodles or
    spinach fettucine
2 tablespoons butter
2 cloves garlic, minced
1½ cups sliced mushrooms
1 pound (450g) spinach, stemmed, well
    washed, and chopped
1 cup sour cream
¼ cup grated Parmesan cheese
2 teaspoons dried basil, or 2 tablespoons
    minced fresh basil leaves
½ teaspoon dried oregano
Pinch of nutmeg
Salt and freshly ground pepper to taste

    Cook the spinach noodles *al dente* and drain
them immediately. In the meantime, melt the
butter in a large skillet until it foams. Add the garlic and mushrooms and sauté over low heat until
the mushrooms are about half done. Add the
spinach, cover, and sauté over low heat until the
spinach has wilted. Add the cooked noodles and
the remaining ingredients and simmer over very
low heat for about 10 minutes.
    4 to 6 servings.

A frog he would a-wooing go,
  Heigh ho! says Rowley,
A frog he would a-wooing go,
Whether his mother would let him
  or no.
With a rowley, powley, gammon
  and spinach,
Heigh ho! says Anthony Rowley.

—Old English Nursery Rhyme

> **"***Music is like spaghetti. If you like spaghetti, you do not eat it morning, noon, and night. You only have it once in a while. It should be kept distant so that you have a real hunger for it.***"**

—Dimitri Mitropoulos,
  quoted by Giuseppe Prezzolini in
  Spaghetti Dinner (1955)

VERMICELLI PRIMAVERA

"Primavera" means spring in Italian, and is also the name of the dish that combines pasta with fresh vegetables. It's a light way to serve pasta and you may substitute other spring vegetables if you like.

½ pound (225g) vermicelli
2 tablespoons butter
½ cup grated Parmesan cheese
2 tablespoons olive oil
3 to 4 cloves garlic, minced
2 cups chopped or sliced mushrooms
1½ cups string beans or asparagus, cut
      into 1-inch (2½ cm) pieces and
      steamed
1½ cups finely chopped broccoli or fresh
      green peas, steamed
2 cups finely chopped cauliflower,
      steamed
1 14-ounce (400g) can imported plum
      tomatoes with liquid, chopped
2 teaspoons paprika
½ teaspoon dried oregano
¼ teaspoon dried thyme
Pinch of dried rosemary
Fresh parsley and/or basil leaves to taste
Salt and freshly ground pepper to taste
Extra grated Parmesan cheese for topping

Cook the vermicelli *al dente,* drain it immediately, and place it in a large, covered casserole dish. Add the butter and Parmesan cheese and toss to melt. Cover.

In the meantime, heat the olive oil in a large skillet. When it is hot, add the garlic and sauté over low heat until golden. Add the mushrooms and cook until they are slightly wilted. Then add the steamed vegetables and the remaining ingredients. Cover and simmer over very low heat for 8 to 10 minutes. Pour over the pasta in the casserole and toss together. Top each serving with extra Parmesan cheese.

4 to 6 servings.

TOMATO-HERB PASTA SAUCE

For those of us who don't have the time to make long-simmering pasta sauces, this quick version will prove very satisfactory. Aside from the fresh parsley, any herbs you can substitute in a 3 to 1 ratio for the dry will make the sauce even better.

2 tablespoons olive oil
2 to 3 cloves garlic, minced
1 14-ounce (400g) can imported plum
 tomatoes with liquid, chopped
2 6-ounce (180g) cans tomato paste
3 tablespoons minced fresh parsley
1 teaspoon dried basil, more or less to
 taste
1 teaspoon dried oregano, more or less
 to taste
1 teaspoon paprika
1/2 teaspoon dried marjoram
1/4 teaspoon dried thyme
Pinch of dried rosemary, optional
Salt and freshly ground pepper to taste

In a large, heavy saucepan, heat the olive oil. When it is hot, add the garlic and sauté over low heat until golden. Add all the remaining ingredients along with 1/4 cup water, stir together and cover. Simmer over very low heat for 15 minutes. Stir occasionally and have the cover on slightly ajar so that the steam can escape. Adjust the consistency with more water if desired.

Makes enough sauce for 4 to 6 servings of pasta.

Variations: Add approximately 2 cups of sautéed vegetables, such as eggplant, zucchini, mushrooms, or a combination; or 2 cups of steamed, chopped broccoli; or 1/2 cup of chopped black olives. In any case, you can also add 1/4 cup of grated Parmesan cheese to the sauce once it is cooked—aside from the extra Parmesan cheese you pass around.

"Don't be intimidated by foreign cookery. Tomatoes and oregano make it Italian. Wine and tarragon make it French. Sour cream makes it Russian. Lemon and cinnamon make it Greek. Soy sauce makes it Chinese. Garlic makes it good. Now you are an International Cook. "

—Alice May Brock
Alice's Restaurant Cookbook (1969)

Basil was once an emblem of love in Italy. A young man wishing to marry his sweetheart might approach her with a sprig of basil in his hair or hat.

FETTUCINE ALFREDO WITH MUSHROOMS AND BASIL

Fresh basil has a wonderful affinity with pasta and presented here are two possibilities for its use, one with the rich classical Alfredo sauce, and the other in a lighter context. Look for fresh basil in late summer and early autumn, when it is sold in large, fragrant bunches in produce stores and farmer's markets.

½ pound (225g) white or green fettucine
1 tablespoon olive oil
½ pound (225g) coarsely chopped mushrooms
1 cup chopped fresh basil leaves
¾ cup heavy cream
1 cup milk
2 to 3 tablespoons butter
3 tablespoons flour
2 egg yolks, beaten
⅓ cup grated Parmesan cheese
Salt and freshly ground pepper to taste

Cook the fettucine *al dente*. When it is done, drain and transfer it to a large casserole with a cover.

Heat the olive oil in a skillet. When it is hot, add the mushrooms and sauté over moderately low heat until tender. If an excessive amount of liquid forms, drain off a bit. Stir in the basil leaves, remove from the heat, and cover.

Heat the cream, milk and butter in a heavy saucepan. Meanwhile, dissolve the flour in just enough water to form a smooth, flowing paste. When the cream and milk mixture is just under the boiling point, pour in the flour paste slowly, stirring constantly with a whisk. Turn to moderately low heat and whisk almost continuously until the mixture thickens. Remove from the heat and quickly whisk in the beaten egg yolks. Then add the grated Parmesan cheese, the mushrooms and basil. Toss with the fettucine, and add salt and freshly ground pepper to taste.

4 to 6 servings.

ROTELLE WITH TOMATOES, ARTICHOKES AND BASIL

Rotelle, a corkscrew-shaped pasta, is an excellent receptacle for the thin but zesty sauce that is formed by the fresh tomatoes, basil, and marinated artichokes. This light and summery pasta dish is a special favorite of mine, and I think anyone who loves fresh basil will really enjoy it.

½ pound (225g) rotelle
1 tablespoon olive oil
1 to 2 cloves garlic, minced
1 medium sweet red or green pepper, cut into julienne strips
1 pound ripe, red tomatoes, diced
½ cup firmly packed chopped fresh basil leaves, more or less to taste
¾ pound (340g) marinated artichoke hearts, either 2 6-ounce (180g) jars or bought by weight
1 tablespoon red wine vinegar
1 teaspoon dried oregano
Salt and freshly ground pepper to taste
1½ cups diced mozzarella or Gruyère cheese, optional

Begin cooking the pasta *al dente*. When it is done, drain and transfer to a serving casserole.

In the meantime, heat the olive oil in a large skillet. When it is hot, add the garlic and green pepper and sauté until the green pepper is softened but not browned. Add the tomatoes and sauté just until they have lost their raw quality. Do not let them soften. Add the remaining ingredients, except for the cheese, and cook until just heated through.

Combine the pasta and the vegetable mixture in your serving casserole and toss together. This is best served warm, not hot, or even at room temperature. Add the diced cheese once the mixture has cooled down, and toss again.

4 to 6 servings.

ναυτια!!
ευαίσθητα
πόδια!
πόνο!!

In ancient Greece, it was believed that unless the sowing of basil was accompanied by cursing or railing, it would not flourish.

VEGETABLE LO MEIN

Since noodles most likely originated in the Orient, there we find some of the most delectable ways to prepare them. Three possibilities are presented on these two pages.

2 tablespoons sesame oil
3 heaping cups broccoli, cut into
**   bite-sized pieces and florets**
1 medium onion, chopped
2 medium celery stalks, sliced diagonally
1 cup firmly packed fresh bean sprouts
1 6- or 8-ounce (180 or 225g) can bamboo
**   shoots**
1¼ cups steamed fresh or (thawed) frozen
**   green peas**
2 to 3 tablespoons chopped cilantro,
**   optional**
½ pound (225g) vermicelli or fine Chinese
**   noodles, broken in half**
1 recipe Basic Chinese Sauce (page 48)
Soy sauce or tamari to taste

Heat the sesame oil and 3 to 4 tablespoons water or vegetable stock in a large skillet or wok. When very hot, turn the heat to moderate and add the broccoli and onion. Stir-fry for 2 to 3 minutes, then add the celery and stir-fry until it is nearly tender-crisp. Add the bean sprouts and stir-fry just until they are wilted. Add the bamboo shoots, peas, and cilantro and remove from the heat.

Cook the noodles *al dente* and drain. Pour the Basic Chinese Sauce over the vegetables and return to moderate heat just until everything is heated through. Combine the vegetables and noodles in a serving casserole and toss well. Add extra soy sauce or tamari to taste.

4 to 6 servings.

COLD SESAME NOODLES

Sesame noodles are quickly becoming a vegetarian favorite. Some recipes call for peanut butter, but I find this rich enough with just the tahini. For a menu suggestion, see Easy Eggs Foo Yong (page 62).

1/2 pound (225g) vermicelli or fine Chinese noodles
1 large celery stalk
1 medium turnip, peeled
1 large carrot
1 tablespoon sesame oil
1 tablespoon soy sauce or tamari
2 cloves garlic, minced

For the sauce:
1/3 cup tahini (sesame paste)
2 tablespoons miso (see note, page 29), dissolved in 1/2 cup lukewarm water
2 teaspoons sesame oil
1 tablespoon honey
2 tablespoons dry white wine or sherry
1 tablespoon rice vinegar or white vinegar
1 teaspoon freshly grated ginger, more or less to taste
Cayenne pepper to taste
2 tablespoons sesame seeds

Cook the noodles *al dente,* then immediately drain them and splash them with cool water. Let them dry somewhat and then transfer them to a serving bowl.

Cut the celery, turnip, and carrot into 1 1/2- to 2-inch long (4 to 5 cm) matchstick-shaped pieces, as narrow as you have the patience to make them. Heat the sesame oil and soy sauce in a skillet. When hot, add the garlic and sauté over low heat until golden. Turn the heat up to moderate and add the celery, turnip, and carrot. Stir-fry just until they have lost their raw quality, but are still quite crisp. Add them to the noodles.

Combine all the sauce ingredients in a small bowl and whisk together until well blended. Use your own discretion with the ginger and cayenne; this dish can be anything from mildly spicy to very fiery depending on how much of each you use. Pour the sauce over the noodles and toss together until the noodles are evenly coated.

4 to 6 servings.

BUCKWHEAT NOODLES WITH SNOW PEAS

Buckwheat is a more extensively used grain in the Far East than in the West, and it is used to make buckwheat noodles, or soba, which have a very pleasant, slightly nutty flavor. Buckwheat noodles have long been popular in Japan, where they were held as a symbol of friendship, festivity, and wealth. It was traditional for Japanese families to eat them on New Year's Eve as an omen of prosperity for the upcoming year. Look for buckwheat noodles in Oriental food stores.

1/2 pound (225g) buckwheat noodles (soba)
2 tablespoons sesame oil
1 large onion, cut in half and sliced
1 large carrot, thinly sliced
1 1/2 to 2 cups snow peas
1 recipe Basic Chinese Sauce (page 48)
Soy sauce or tamari to taste

Break the noodles in half and cook them *al dente.* Watch them carefully, as they cook rather quickly. Drain and splash with cool water. Drain again and set aside.

Heat the sesame oil in a large skillet or wok. Stir-fry the onion and carrot over moderate to moderately high heat until they are tender-crisp. Add the snow peas and stir-fry just until they have lost their raw quality but are still quite crisp.

Add the noodles and Basic Chinese Sauce to the skillet and toss together with the vegetables. Heat just until everything is thoroughly heated through. Serve with extra soy sauce or tamari.

4 to 6 servings.

The word "vegetable" is one of the vaguest in the culinary vocabulary. The Merriam-Webster dictionary defines a vegetable as a "usually herbaceous plant grown for an edible part that is usually eaten with the principle course of a meal."

When Dr. William Alcott declared that "a vegetable diet lies at the basis of all reform," it is safe to assume that he was speaking of anything edible in the plant kingdom, and that includes grains, legumes, and nuts, yet these are not defined as vegetables, although they may in some way fit the dictionary definition. To add to the confusion, some vegetables are actually fruits botanically, including tomatoes, cucumbers, and the squash family, the latter of which are closely related to the melon family. Just as some vegetables are the fruits of a plant, others derive from differing parts of plants— cauliflower and broccoli are flowers, cabbage and the lettuces are leaves, asparagus is a stalk, carrots and turnips are roots.

So, while we do have a pretty clear idea of what we consider to be vegetables, it is more difficult to actually define what one is. A battle over this question once went all the way to the U.S. Supreme Court—more on that later in this chapter. In this chapter you will find recipes that concentrate on a select group of vegetables, garnished with some of their fascinating histories.

"Opinyuns are jist like any other kind ov vegetable— worth jist what they will fetch. "

—Josh Billings
Josh Billings' Farmer's Alminax (ca. 1870)

HERBED VEGETABLE BREAD LOAF

Nothing enhances the flavor of vegetables like herbs, as the recipes on these two pages will attest.

3 tablespoons butter
1 medium carrot, cut into quarters lengthwise and sliced
2 cloves garlic, minced
1 medium sweet red or green pepper, finely chopped
1 medium zucchini, peeled and finely diced
4 eggs, beaten
2 tablespoons milk
1 cup cooked fresh or (thawed) frozen corn kernels
1 cup string beans, cut into ½-inch (1½ cm) pieces and steamed
4 average slices whole grain bread, cut into ½-inch-square (1½ cm) pieces
¼ cup chopped green olives, optional
2 tablespoons minced fresh parsley
1 tablespoon minced chives
½ teaspoon each: dried thyme, oregano, summer savory and marjoram, ground cumin, and dry mustard
Wheat germ or sunflower seeds for topping

Preheat the oven to 350°F (180°C).

Heat the butter in a skillet until it foams. Add the carrot and garlic and sauté over moderately low heat until the vegetables are golden. Add the red or green pepper and zucchini and sauté until they are just tender.

In a mixing bowl, beat the eggs well with the milk. Add all the remaining ingredients and mix thoroughly. Pour into an oiled, 9- by 5-inch (23 by 13 cm) loaf pan, sprinkle with wheat germ and bake for 50 minutes, or until eggs are set and the top is nicely browned. Let stand for 10 minutes before serving. Cut into slices to serve.

4 to 6 servings.

KUKU SABZI
(PERSIAN SPINACH AND FRESH HERBS PIE)

Persian Kukus are more or less like frittatas, and may be baked as well as made in a skillet. I like to make this version in a skillet, as it tastes best to me in the summer, when I avoid baking. Some time is required in preparation, with all the stemming and chopping, but it is an unusual treat for those who love the strong flavor of fresh herbs.

1 pound (450g) fresh spinach, stemmed, well washed, and chopped
3/4 cup chopped fresh parsley or 1/2 cup chopped fresh parsley and 1/4 cup chopped fresh basil leaves
1/4 cup chopped fresh dill (use a little less if you're unaccustomed to fresh dill—its flavor becomes very distinct here)
3 bunches scallions, chopped
3 eggs
1/2 cup bread crumbs or matzo meal
Salt and freshly ground pepper to taste
1 teaspoon good curry powder or Home-Mixed Curry (page 170), optional

In a large skillet with a cover, steam the spinach until it is wilted but still bright green. You may have to do this half at a time. Transfer the steamed spinach to a colander and squeeze out as much liquid as possible.

Place the spinach in a mixing bowl and add to it all the fresh herbs, including the scallions. Break the eggs right into the mixture, then add all the remaining ingredients and mix thoroughly. To cook, follow the instructions for "How to Fry and Flip a Skillet Pie or Frittata" on page 180. Cut into wedges to serve.

4 to 6 servings.

"*Much virtue in herbs, little in men.* **"**

—Benjamin Franklin
Poor Richard's Almanack (1734)

Dill   Anethum graveolens, C.

Virtues: An herb of savor and beauty, it soothes the stomach, cures hiccoughs, and works against witch craft. For cookery, there are few herbs more welcome than dill.

Boris Clary   Homo Sapiens

Virtues: Rarely smokes and tells lies infrequently.

BROCCOLI BREAD PUDDING

This simple but deliciously rich way to use broccoli has become a special occasion standard among my family since guests really seem to love it.

2 tablespoons butter
1 large onion, chopped
1 clove garlic, minced
4 cups finely chopped broccoli, steamed
1 cup sour cream
2 teaspoons mixed dried herbs of your
choice, optional
Salt and freshly ground pepper to taste
4 eggs, beaten
¼ cup milk
4 average slices whole grain bread
2 cups grated mild cheese
Wheat germ plus sesame seeds
for topping

Preheat the oven to 350°F (180°C).

Heat the butter in a large skillet until it begins to foam. Add the onion and garlic and sauté over moderately low heat until the onion is nicely browned. Add the broccoli, sour cream, herbs, and salt and pepper. Stir together and remove from the heat.

Beat together the eggs and the milk. Tear the bread into small pieces. Oil a deep, 9- by 9-inch (23 by 23 cm) casserole dish and layer as follows: half the bread, half the broccoli mixture, half the eggs, and half the cheese. Repeat the layers, then sprinkle with first the wheat germ and then the sesame seeds. Bake for 35 to 40 minutes, or until the top is nicely browned.

4 to 6 servings.

Broccoli is native to Italy (it means "little sprouts" in Italian), and its cookery dates back to the epicure of classical Rome, Apicius, who gave the world one of its first recorded cookbooks. The controversial Roman emperor Tiberius was reported to have seriously scolded his son Drusus for overindulging in broccoli.

STIR-FRIED ALMOND BROCCOLI AND CAULIFLOWER

Broccoli and cauliflower are both members of the cabbage family, and they not only complement each other's flavor, they look very attractive together. This quick and simple combination of the two can be done in a skillet if it's 10 inches (25 cm) or so, but is easier done in a wok.

2 tablespoons sesame oil
2 cloves garlic, minced
4 tablespoons dry sherry or dry white wine
2 tablespoons soy sauce or tamari
3 heaping cups broccoli, cut into
bite-sized pieces and florets
3 heaping cups cauliflower, cut into
bite-sized pieces and florets
⅓ cup finely chopped almonds

Heat 1 tablespoon of the sesame oil in the skillet or wok. When it is hot, add the garlic and sauté over low heat for a minute or so. Add the remaining oil, the sherry, and soy sauce. Turn the heat to moderate and add the broccoli and cauliflower. Stir quickly to coat them with the liquid. Stir-fry until they are just tender-crisp. Add the chopped almonds and stir-fry just until the pieces are well distributed. Serve as soon as possible.

4 to 6 servings.

CAULIFLOWER AVOCADO BAKE

1 large head cauliflower
2 eggs, well beaten
Salt and freshly ground pepper to taste
1 medium ripe avocado, peeled and cut into small dice
2 tablespoons butter
1 medium sweet red or green pepper, cut into julienne strips
2 to 3 bunches scallions, chopped
3 tablespoons finely chopped fresh parsley
1 cup firmly packed grated mild cheese
Sesame seeds for topping

Preheat the oven to 350°F (180°C).

Cut the cauliflower into bite-sized pieces and florets and steam or stir-fry until tender-crisp. In a large bowl, stir together the beaten eggs, salt and pepper, and the cooked cauliflower until it is evenly coated with the eggs. Oil a large, shallow baking dish and arrange the cauliflower pieces in it. Sprinkle the diced avocado over the cauliflower.

Heat the butter in a skillet until it foams. Add the red or green pepper and sauté over moderately low heat until it softens a bit, then add the scallions and parsley and sauté until they are wilted. Spread this mixture evenly over the cauliflower and avocado, and top with the grated cheese. Sprinkle the sesame seeds generously over the top. Bake for 20 minutes.

4 to 6 servings.

"*Training is everything. The peach was once a bitter almond; cauliflower is nothing but cabbage with a college education.*"

—Mark Twain
Pudd'nhead Wilson (1896)

MUSHROOM BREAD PUDDING

1 tablespoon butter
1 pound (450g) mushrooms, sliced
3 eggs, well beaten
1 cup sour cream
1/2 cup grated Parmesan cheese
1/2 teaspoon dried basil
1/4 teaspoon dried thyme
1/4 teaspoon dried summer savory
Salt and freshly ground pepper to taste
Fresh French or Italian bread, as needed,
    cut into 1/2-inch-thick (1 1/2 cm) slices

Preheat the oven to 325°F (165°C).

Heat the butter in a large skillet until it foams. Add the mushrooms and sauté over moderately low heat until the mushrooms are just tender. Remove from the heat and drain off any liquid that the mushrooms may have given off.

In a mixing bowl, beat the eggs until bubbly, then stir the sour cream into them. Add the mushrooms and all the remaining ingredients, except the bread, and mix thoroughly.

Oil a deep, 9- by 9-inch (23 by 23 cm) casserole dish and line the bottom completely with a single layer of the sliced bread. Pour half of the mushroom mixture evenly over it. Repeat with the remaining bread and mushroom mixture.

Bake for 25 minutes.

4 to 6 servings.

When the moon is at the full,
*   Mushrooms you may freely pull,*
But when the moon is on the wane,
*   Wait ere you think to pluck again.*

—Old English Rhyme

MUSHROOMS AND TOFU IN WINE

A friend devised this quick dish which abounds in mushrooms. Her idea of grating the tofu is excellent, because the tofu then really absorbs all the flavors of the aromatic sauce. I highly recommend this to anyone who loves mushrooms.

1 tablespoon safflower or vegetable oil
2 cloves garlic, minced
1 large onion, chopped
1½ pounds (675g) mushrooms, sliced or
    coarsely chopped
½ medium green pepper, finely chopped
½ cup dry white wine
¼ cup soy sauce or tamari
½ teaspoon freshly grated ginger
2 teaspoons sesame oil
1½ tablespoons cornstarch
2 cakes tofu (bean curd), coarsely grated
Crushed almonds or crisp Chinese noodles
    for garnish

Heat the oil in a large skillet. When it is hot, add the garlic and onion and sauté over moderately low heat until the onion is translucent.

Add the mushrooms, green pepper, wine, soy sauce, ginger, and sesame oil to the skillet and stir together. Turn the heat down to low, cover, and simmer until the mushrooms are tender but not overdone.

Dissolve the cornstarch in a small amount of water and stir it into the skillet. Stir in the grated tofu, cover, and simmer for 2 or 3 minutes longer, or until the liquid has thickened. Serve over grains or noodles, garnished with crushed almonds or crisp Chinese noodles.

4 to 6 servings.

Mushrooms which today are considered almost a delicacy, had to overcome a bad reputation of long standing. They were considered a wicked food, as these two seventeenth-century writers will attest:

"Many have eaten and do eat mushrooms more for wantonnesse than for neede... "

—John Gerarde
The Herball (1636)

"I have the same opinion of dances that physicians have of mushrooms: the best of them are good for nothing. "

—St. Francis de Sales
Introduction to the
Devout Life (1609)

Fairies and other sprites had a strong affinity with mushrooms, having often been seen dancing, cavorting, or just resting around them. Perhaps this association with the impish creatures fueled the notion that mushrooms meant mischief.

Few people I know dislike eggplant, yet as with mushrooms, it has had a very turbulent history, as evidenced by the variety of strange names it has had. In Italian, it is called "melanzana," a corruption of the ancient Latin "mala insana," which translated into English as Raging Apple or Mad Apple. John Gerarde in his *Herball* (1636) concluded that "...doubtless these Apples have a mischievous qualitie, the use whereof is utterly to be forsaken."

In the Bible, the Apple of Sodom was a large purple eggplant. Its outward beauty was deceptive, for its fruit would turn to ash on the lips of anyone who tried to partake of it—and thereby was a symbol of sin.

EGGPLANT-RICOTTA "SANDWICHES"

Eggplant slices filled with ricotta cheese make a nice change of pace from Eggplant Parmigiana.

½ pound (225g) ricotta cheese
¼ cup grated Parmesan cheese
1 egg yolk
½ teaspoon salt
2 medium eggplants, more round than long
1 recipe Tomato-Herb Pasta Sauce, eliminating 1 of the 6-ounce (180g) cans tomato paste (page 107)
1½ cups grated mozzarella cheese

Combine the first 4 ingredients in a small bowl, mix well and set aside.

Peel and slice each eggplant crosswise into 8 slices. Broil several slices at a time, brushed with a little oil, in the broiler of your oven, until both sides are lightly browned. Turn the oven to 350°F (180°C).

Oil one or two shallow baking dishes, as needed, and pour in just enough Tomato-Herb Sauce to coat the bottom. Make "sandwiches" by spreading the ricotta mixture on one eggplant slice and covering it with another slice of the same size. Arrange in the baking dishes, top with the remaining sauce, and sprinkle with the grated cheese.

Bake for 30 to 35 minutes, or until the eggplants are done to your liking.

4 servings.

CUSTARD-TOPPED EGGPLANT AND BULGUR BAKE

I have to admit that this recipe may have a "mischievous qualitie," since it is somewhat rich and takes some time to prepare, but it is a very attractive and delicious way to serve eggplant for special occasions.

1 cup raw bulgur
2 tablespoons soy sauce or tamari
2 medium eggplants (choose ones that are long rather than round)
3 eggs
1 cup heavy cream
2 cloves garlic, minced
3 bunches scallions, chopped
1 teaspoon dried marjoram
1/4 teaspoon dried thyme
1 pound very ripe tomatoes, chopped, or 1 14-ounce (400g) can imported plum tomatoes, lightly drained and chopped
2 tablespoons finely chopped fresh parsley
1 cup grated mozzarella cheese

Bring 2 cups of water to a boil, then pour over the bulgur in a bowl. Stir in the soy sauce or tamari, cover, and let stand until the water is absorbed, about 30 minutes.

Slice the eggplants into 1/2-inch-thick (1 1/2 cm) slices and peel them, if you'd like. Arrange several at a time in your oven's broiler, brush with a little oil, and broil on both sides until lightly browned. When this is done, turn the oven to 350°F (180°C).

Beat 2 of the eggs until bubbly, then whisk in the cream until well blended.

Lightly beat the last egg and mix it into the bulgur, then stir in the garlic (if you'd like a subtler garlic flavor, sauté it in a little oil until golden before adding), scallion, marjoram, and thyme.

Layer in a large, shallow, oiled casserole dish as follows: All the bulgur, patted in smoothly; the eggplant overlapped in rows; the chopped tomatoes and parsley; the egg-cream mixture; and the grated cheese.

Bake for 35 to 40 minutes, or until the custard is set, the eggplant is tender, and the cheese is browned.

6 servings.

EGGPLANT SKILLET PIE

These herbed eggplant wedges make a perfect accompaniment, along with a mixed fresh vegetable salad to many types of pasta dishes. Try this with either of the two pasta and fresh basil recipes (pages 108 and 109).

2 tablespoons olive oil
1 medium eggplant, peeled and diced
1 clove garlic, crushed or minced
3 eggs, lightly beaten
1/2 cup bread crumbs or a combination of bread crumbs and wheat germ
1/2 teaspoon dried basil
1/2 teaspoon dried marjoram
1/4 teaspoon dried oregano
1/4 teaspoon dried thyme
Salt and freshly ground pepper to taste

Heat the olive oil in a large skillet. When it is hot, add the eggplant and a small quantity of water. Cover and cook over low heat. Stir occasionally and add just enough water to keep the eggplant from sticking. Cook until the eggplant is quite soft, then transfer it to a mixing bowl.

Mash the eggplant well with a potato masher or a fork. Add the remaining ingredients and mix thoroughly. To cook, follow the directions for "How to Fry and Flip a Skillet Pie or Frittata" on page 180.

Cut into 6 wedges to serve.

ZUCCHINI PANCAKES PARMESAN

Zucchini is one of the few squashes that is not native to the Americas. It was developed in Italy.

4 cups firmly packed coarsely grated zucchini
3 eggs, well beaten
½ cup matzo meal or bread crumbs
½ teaspoon dried dill
½ teaspoon dried marjoram
¼ teaspoon dried thyme
Salt and freshly ground pepper to taste
½ cup grated Parmesan cheese
Oil for frying

Place the grated zucchini in a colander for several minutes and squeeze out the moisture.

Beat the eggs well in a mixing bowl, add to them the remaining ingredients and mix thoroughly.

You can fry these in one of two ways—either as palm-sized croquettes in a large skillet, or as crêpe-sized pancakes in a small, 7-inch (18 cm) or so skillet. In either case, heat just enough oil to coat the bottom of the skillet, and when it is hot enough to make a drop of batter sizzle, proceed to fry in whatever manner you've decided until both sides are nicely browned and crisp looking. Drain on paper towels.

Makes about 20 palm-sized or 8 to 10 crêpe-sized pancakes.

Squash is truly a food of the Americas. Its name is possibly a corruption of "askoot-asquash," meaning "the fruit that is yellow" in an Indian dialect. Squash in its numerous varieties originated with the pre-Incan Indians thousands of years ago. Along with pumpkin, it was so abundant when the European settlers reached North America that it could sometimes drive pioneer wives like this to despair. By itself, squash may perhaps be monotonous, but with a little imagination, it is a most interesting, versatile vegetable.

"O dear! How can I tell it. Squash again for breakfast."

—Diary of a Pioneer Woman

122

SPAGHETTI SQUASH WITH BROCCOLI-ASPARAGUS PESTO

If you like pesto on pasta, why not try one on spaghetti squash? Of course, if you like this pesto, there's no reason not to use it on pasta as well. This is a pleasing way to serve a very enjoyable squash.

1 large spaghetti squash
2 to 3 tablespoons butter
Salt and freshly ground pepper to taste

For the pesto:
2 tablespoons olive oil
2 cloves garlic, minced
1 cup walnuts
½ cup grated Parmesan cheese
2 cups chopped steamed broccoli
1½ cups chopped steamed asparagus
¼ cup milk or light cream
1 egg yolk
1 teaspoon dried oregano
Salt and freshly ground pepper to taste
A few fresh basil leaves, optional

Preheat the oven to 350°F (180°C).

Cut the squash in half; remove the seeds and pulp. (You can clean the seeds and roast them—they are just like pumpkin seeds.) Place the squash halves, cut side down, in a shallow baking pan with ¼ inch (⅔ cm) of water and bake for 40 to 45 minutes. When cool enough to handle, pull the spaghetti-like strands off the squash with a fork, using long vertical motions. Heat the butter in a large skillet until it begins to foam, then add the spaghetti squash and sauté over low heat. Season with salt and pepper and toss until the squash is evenly coated with the butter. Remove from heat and cover.

To prepare the pesto, heat the olive oil in a small skillet. When it is hot, add the garlic and sauté over low heat until golden.

Place the walnuts in the workbowl of a food processor or blender and process until finely ground. Add the garlic along with all the remaining ingredients and process until a smooth, thick purée is achieved. Warm the purée in a heavy saucepan but do not let it boil. Spoon over the spaghetti squash and serve.

4 to 6 servings.

SUMMER HARVEST SQUASH SAUTÉ

At the end of the summer, and throughout most of the autumn, many enticing squashes are on display. Green, yellow, and orange squashes look very appealing together in this quick sauté with greens.

1 small butternut squash
3 tablespoons butter
1 large yellow summer squash, peeled, halved lengthwise, and sliced
1 large zucchini, halved lengthwise, and sliced
2 tablespoons dry white or red wine
2 tablespoons soy sauce or tamari
3 cups chopped greens, such as spinach or swiss chard
½ teaspoon dried summer savory
½ teaspoon dried marjoram
¼ teaspoon dried dill
Freshly ground pepper to taste

To prepare the butternut squash, halve it lengthwise and remove the seeds and pulp. Then cut crosswise into slices, about 1 inch (2½ cm) wide. Peel and then cut into fairly thin slices.

Heat 2 tablespoons of the butter with 2 tablespoons of water in a large skillet. When the butter is melted add the butternut squash, cover, and steam over low heat, stirring occasionally for 10 minutes, or until the squash seems about half done. Add the summer squash and the zucchini, adding a little more water if necessary, and cook over moderately low heat, stirring frequently, until the squashes are done to your liking.

Add the remaining butter, the wine and soy sauce and stir together. Stir in the greens, cover the skillet, and cook until they are wilted. Add the seasonings and serve.

6 servings.

Variations: To make this a main dish, add two cakes of diced tofu before removing the skillet from the heat, allowing them to heat through. Serve over grains. Or, arrange in a baking dish, top with some grated cheese, and bake in a hot oven just until the cheese melts, and serve over grains. Serve with extra soy sauce or tamari.

GINGERED RICE AND APPLE STUFFED SQUASH

2 medium acorn or butternut squashes
¾ cup raw brown rice
2 tablespoons soy sauce or tamari
2 tablespoons butter
1 small onion, chopped
2 medium apples, peeled, cored, and sliced
⅓ cup chopped walnuts, almonds, or pecans
½ cup light cream or milk
¼ cup dry red wine
2 tablespoons honey
2 teaspoons freshly grated ginger, more or less to taste
1 teaspoon good curry powder or Home-Mixed Curry (page 170)
½ teaspoon nutmeg
1 cup grated mild white cheese, optional

Preheat the oven to 350°F (180°C).

Cut the squashes in half, place them cut side up on flat baking sheets, and cover them with aluminum foil. Bake for about 35 to 45 minutes, or until tender.

In the meantime, cook the rice with the soy sauce added to the cooking water (see Cooking Grains on page 178).

When the squash is cool enough to handle, scoop out the pulp, leaving about a ½ inch (1½ cm) shell of pulp all around. Chop the pulp and set aside.

Heat the butter in a large skillet until it foams. Add the onion and sauté over moderately low heat until it is translucent. Add the apple and sauté until it softens, then add the squash pulp, cooked rice, and the remaining ingredients. Stir together and remove from the heat.

Stuff the squash halves with the rice mixture, arrange in lightly oiled baking dishes, and bake for 20 minutes.

4 servings.

"Ginger sharpneth the sight, and provoketh slothful husbands."

—William Vaughn
Directions for Health (1600)

DILLED CARROT CROQUETTES

Fresh dill wonderfully enhances the flavor of carrots, whether they serveth in love matters or not. Dried dill is acceptable to substitute if it has a fresh scent.

2 cups very firmly packed, coarsely grated carrot
2 eggs, beaten
1 small onion, grated
⅓ cup plain yogurt
⅓ cup bread crumbs, or a combination of crumbs with wheat germ or cornmeal
3 tablespoons finely chopped fresh dill or 1½ tablespoons dried dill
1 teaspoon dried summer savory
¾ teaspoon ground coriander
Salt and freshly ground pepper to taste
Safflower or vegetable oil for frying

Combine all the ingredients, except the oil, in a mixing bowl and mix thoroughly.

Heat just enough oil to coat the bottom of a large skillet. Shape the mixture into palm-sized croquettes and fry over low heat on both sides until nicely browned. Drain on paper towels.

Makes about 12 croquettes.

"*The carrot serveth for love matters; and Orpheus, as Pliny writeth, said that the use therof winneth love...* **"**

—John Gerarde
The Herball (1636)

ARTICHOKE HEARTS
IN WHITE CHEESE SAUCE

This recipe is for those, like me, who like artichoke hearts but dread working with whole artichokes. A major packager of artichoke hearts, Cara Mia, provides frozen artichoke hearts that are very good and relatively inexpensive.

1 tablespoon olive oil
2 cloves garlic, minced
⅓ cup chopped fresh parsley
1 recipe White Cheese Sauce (page 49)
1 10-ounce (285g) package frozen artichoke hearts, thawed, drained and cut into bite-sized pieces
Juice of ½ lemon
¼ cup toasted sunflower seeds
1 teaspoon dried summer savory
2 hard-boiled eggs, chopped
Salt and freshly ground pepper to taste

Heat the olive oil in a large skillet. When it is hot, add the garlic and sauté over low heat for 1 minute. Add the parsley and sauté just until the garlic is golden and the parsley is slightly wilted.

Add the remaining ingredients and simmer over very low heat for 10 minutes. Serve on its own or over pasta or grains, especially couscous.

4 servings.

"*When [artichokes] be almost rype, they must be sodden tender... and after eate them at dyner, they both increase nature and doth provoke a man to veneryous actes.* **"**

—Dr. Andrew Boorde
A Compendyous Regyment or a Dyetary of Healthe (1567)

There are few things more useful in vegetable cookery than tomatoes. Cultivated by the Indians of the Americas, tomatoes reached Europe via the Spanish after their sixteenth-century conquest of Mexico. From there the tomato traveled all over Europe under many interesting names. In Italy, it was first called "pomo dei mori," apple of the Moors, then "pomo d'oro," golden apple. In France and Germany it was considered an aphrodisiac and thus was called, respectively, "pomme d'amour" and "liebesapfel," both meaning apple of love. From England the tomato traveled back to the American colonies, where until the early nineteenth century it was considered poisonous, being related to the deadly nightshade. As late as 1860, the apprehension lingered, as evidenced by a recipe in Godey's Lady's Book which recommended cooking tomatoes for at least three hours before eating.

TOMATOES STUFFED WITH CURRIED EGGPLANT

One of the most common yet still very interesting ways to highlight the tomato is to stuff it with tasty mixtures. Here are two possibilities.

6 large, firm but ripe tomatoes
1 medium eggplant, on the smaller side
2 tablespoons safflower or vegetable oil
2 cloves garlic, minced
½ cup plain yogurt
¼ cup wheat germ or bread crumbs
3 tablespoons chopped cilantro or
**   fresh parsley**
1½ to 2 teaspoons good curry powder or
**   Home-Mixed Curry (page 170)**
Salt and freshly ground pepper to taste

Preheat the oven to 350°F (180°C).

Cut each tomato in half, carefully scooping out the pulp with the aid of a knife and spoon. Reserve the chopped pulp in a bowl. Arrange the tomato halves in an oiled, large shallow baking dish.

Peel the eggplant and cut it into small dice. Heat the oil and ¼ cup of water in a large skillet. When hot, add the eggplant and garlic, cover, and cook until the eggplant is tender, stirring occasionally and adding enough water to keep it from sticking. Remove from the heat. Add the tomato pulp and all the remaining ingredients and mix thoroughly. Stuff each tomato half with the mixture.

Bake for 30 to 35 minutes, or until the tomatoes are done to your liking.

6 servings.

TOMATOES STUFFED WITH ORZO AND PEAS

What goes better with tomatoes than pasta? The tiny size and pleasant texture of orzo suits these stuffed tomatoes just right.

6 large, firm but ripe tomatoes
2/3 cup raw orzo (rice-shaped pasta)
2 tablespoons butter
2 tablespoons minced fresh parsley
2 tablespoons minced fresh chives
2/3 cup steamed fresh or (thawed) frozen green peas
2 tablespoons grated Parmesan cheese
1 teaspoon paprika
1/2 teaspoon dried summer savory
1/2 teaspoon dried marjoram
1/2 teaspoon dried basil
Salt and freshly ground pepper to taste
Extra grated Parmesan cheese for topping

Preheat the oven to 350°F (180°C). Prepare the tomatoes in the same way as specified in the previous recipe.

Cook the orzo *al dente,* and drain immediately. Splash with cool water.

Heat the butter in a large skillet until it foams. Add the reserved tomato pulp, parsley, and chives and sauté over low heat until the tomatoes are softened, but do not reduce them to a liquid. Add the peas, Parmesan cheese, seasonings, and orzo. Stir together until thoroughly mixed and remove from heat.

Stuff each tomato half and sprinkle generously with extra Parmesan cheese. Bake for 30 to 35 minutes, or until the tomatoes are done to your liking.

6 servings.

The argument over whether the tomato is a fruit or a vegetable once went all the way to the U.S. Supreme Court. According to the Tarriff Act of 1883, fruits could be imported duty free but vegetables could not. In 1886, one importer argued that since tomatoes were botanically fruits, he should be able to bring them in duty free. The Supreme Court handed down its decision in 1893, judging that although tomatoes are a fruit of the vine, as are squashes, beans, and the like, they as "all those vegetables...are usually served at dinner...and not, like fruits generally, as a dessert." Thus, tomatoes were pronounced vegetables by law.

After "Jurisprudence"
by Daniel Chester French

"Oh, I must try some, if it is an Indian dish," said Miss Rebecca. "I am sure everything must be good that comes from there."

"Give Miss Sharp some curry, my dear," said Mr. Sedley, laughing.

Rebecca had never tasted the dish before.

"Do you find it as good as everything else from India?" said Mr. Sedley.

"Oh, excellent!" said Rebecca, who was suffering tortures with cayenne pepper.

"Try a chili with it, Miss Sharp," said Joseph, really interested.

"A chili," said Rebecca, gasping. "Oh, yes!" She thought a chili was something cool, as its name imported, and was served with some. "How fresh and green they look," she said, and put one into her mouth. It was hotter than the curry; flesh and blood could bear it no longer. She laid down her fork. "Water, for Heaven's Sake, water!"

—William Makepeace Thackeray
Vanity Fair (1848)

Menu for an Indian-style Curry Feast:
CURRIED MIXED VEGETABLES (page 128) with grains
SAMOSAS (page 145)
TOMATO APPLE CHUTNEY (page 129)
CUCUMBER RAITA (page 38)
BANANA RAITA (page 163)
Fresh Fruit

_ CURRIED MIXED VEGETABLES _

Just short of buying your spices whole, then roasting and grinding them as Indian cooks do, you can give your curries a wonderfully complex flavor by mixing ground curry spices rather than using dull commercial curry powder. Begin with Home-Mixed Curry as a spice base, and embellish it with additional seasonings, plus fresh ginger and garlic. Use the amounts given here as a guideline (these will give you a moderately spicy result); the degree of spiciness in a curry is very much a matter of personal taste.

**2 tablespoons safflower or vegetable oil
1 large onion, chopped
1 large carrot, thinly sliced
1 medium eggplant, peeled and diced
2 cloves garlic, minced
2 cups cauliflower florets, steamed
3/4 cup string beans, cut into 1-inch (2½cm) pieces and steamed
3/4 cup steamed fresh or (thawed) frozen green peas
1½ 14-ounce (400g) cans imported plum tomatoes with liquid, chopped
1 teaspoon freshly grated ginger
2 tablespoons soy sauce or tamari
2½ to 3 teaspoons Home-Mixed Curry (page 170), more or less to taste, or good curry powder
½ teaspoon ground turmeric
½ teaspoon dry mustard
½ teaspoon cinnamon**

You will need at least a 10-inch (25 cm) skillet for this, or you can use a wok.

Heat the oil. When it is hot, add the onion, carrot, eggplant, and garlic and ¼ cup water. Cover and cook over low heat, stirring occasionally, until the vegetables are nearly tender. Add all the remaining vegetables and seasonings and mix well. Simmer over very low heat for 20 minutes. The vegetables should be more tender than for a stir-fry, but not overdone. Adjust the seasonings. Serve over grains—rice, millet, or couscous are particularly good.

6 servings.

INSTANT TOMATO AND APPLE CHUTNEY

A chutney is a spicy relish served with Indian curries. Many chutneys are actually pickles, which must be stored in sterilized jars for weeks before they can be eaten. Some, though, can be made and eaten immediately, like this easy sweet and spicy version.

1 tablespoon butter
1 medium onion, chopped
2 cloves garlic, minced
2 medium sweet apples, peeled, cored, and diced
1 pound very ripe, red tomatoes, chopped, or 1 14-ounce (400g) can imported plum tomatoes with liquid, chopped
1 tablespoon honey
1 tablespoon soy sauce or tamari
1 teaspoon freshly grated ginger, more or less to taste
1 teaspoon ground cumin
1/2 teaspoon cinnamon
1/4 teaspoon cayenne pepper or crushed red pepper, more or less to taste
1/4 cup currants or raisins, optional

Heat the butter in a large skillet until it foams. Add the onion and garlic and sauté until the onion is translucent. Add the apples, the tomatoes if you're using fresh, the honey, and the soy sauce. Cover and cook on low heat for 10 minutes, stirring once or twice.

If you're using canned tomatoes, add them at this point, along with the remaining ingredients. The ginger and cayenne or crushed red pepper are what will determine the degree of spiciness. This is intended to be spicy, but be conservative at first, and add small amounts of those two spices to your discretion. Once everything is in the skillet, simmer, uncovered, over very low heat for about 20 minutes, or until the tomatoes are reduced to a loose sauce. Taste and adjust the seasonings.

Makes about 6 servings or more as a relish.

> *"…We [the Chinese] eat food for its texture, the elastic or crisp effect it has on our teeth, as well for fragrance, flavor, and color…The idea of texture is seldom understood, but a great part of the popularity of bamboo shoots is due to the fine resistance the young shoots give to our teeth."*
>
> —Lin Yutang
> *My Country and My People* (1938)

The sixth-century philosopher Lao-Tzu liked to experiment with plant foods and taught his followers that overcooking vegetables destroyed their nutrients. The Taoists based their diets on raw or partially cooked vegetables and it was this tradition that may have led to the art of stir-frying. Stir-fried vegetables, just barely done, are at the height of their color and look as appealing as they taste. Prepared in complementary combinations, each vegetable retains its unique flavor and character in the texture that has come to be known as "tender-crisp."

Menu for a Chinese-style Banquet:

"BUDDHA'S DELIGHT" or SWEET
    AND SOUR VEGETABLES
    (pages 130-131) with rice, cous-
    cous, or noodles
EGGS AND TOFU IN PEANUT
    SAUCE (page 62)
SUNFLOWER COLESLAW (page 35)
PINEAPPLE AND ORANGES IN
    YOGURT (page 164)
Almond Cookies

"BUDDHA'S DELIGHT"
(STIR-FRIED MIXED VEGETABLES)

"Buddha's Delight" was inspired by dishes of the same name on Chinese restaurant menus. Often it is one of the few things on the menu that a vegetarian can order, but it is never exactly the same at any two places, and is almost always quite delicious. Putting together a colorful stir-fry at home is relatively easy and quick; it is one of my personal favorites. If you are making this for guests, have the vegetables cut, but don't start frying until about 25 minutes before you want to eat this course, as it is best eaten when the vegetables are at their brightest and crispest.

Unless you have an extra large skillet, perhaps 14 inches, and you are doing this for more than 2 or 3 people, it is easier done in a wok. The really tricky part of this is that everything has to be ready all at once, so the last 5 to 10 minutes of preparation can be a bit hectic.

First, think of what you'd like to serve the vegetables on. Here are some possibilities:

Brown rice *(Have it ready before starting, then heat through as needed before serving. See Cooking Grains, page 178.)*

Fine Chinese noodles, buckwheat noodles, or vermicelli *(Start cooking these at the same time you prepare your sauce.)*

Couscous *(An offbeat possibility; begin preparing it right before you begin stir-frying. See Cooking Grains, page 178.)*

As for the vegetables, you will need up to 3 heaping cups of cut, raw vegetables per serving, that being a general guideline for healthy appetites. Choose from among the following vegetables, using anywhere from 6 to 9 different ones, and try to select at least 2 per category for a variety of textures. Always use fresh vegetables, except for those specified as canned, since those are generally not available otherwise:

Hard vegetables:
broccoli (cut into approximately 2-inch florets)
cauliflower (cut as above)
carrot (sliced)
onion (chopped or cut into rings)
celery (sliced diagonally)

Medium vegetables:
cabbage (shredded)
sweet red or green pepper (diced)
bok choy (sliced diagonally)
turnips (sliced fairly thin, and cut into strips)

Soft vegetables:
snow peas (stemmed)
mung bean sprouts
mushrooms
scallions
cilantro (chopped)
canned baby corn
canned water chestnuts (sliced)
canned bamboo shoots

Before beginning to stir-fry, assemble and set aside all the ingredients for:

1 recipe Basic Chinese Sauce (page 48).

This recipe is based on 4 to 6 servings, so cut or increase accordingly. Make only as much as you need. The sauce contains the basic flavorings, such as fresh ginger and garlic, and soy sauce or tamari. If you'd like, try the "hot and spicy" variation.

To begin stir-frying, place in the skillet or wok the following (again based on 4 to 6 servings):

1 tablespoon sesame oil
2 tablespoons safflower or vegetable oil
2 tablespoons water

Heat these together over moderately high heat. When really hot, place your "hard" vegetables in the skillet or wok and fry, stirring continuously. Add the "medium" vegetables when the first batch are about halfway to tender-crisp. The ones in the "soft" category have to be just wilted or heated through at the end. After doing this once, you will have a good feeling for when the vegetables should be added in relation to one another. Keep stirring continuously as they fry, until all the vegetables are tender-crisp.

Once the vegetables are done, turn off the heat and leave uncovered while preparing the Basic Chinese Sauce according to recipe. When it is done, pour over the vegetables, and just heat through over moderately high heat. Serve immediately.

SWEET AND SOUR VEGETABLES

Follow the instructions for the stir-fry. Include within the measurements for your vegetables 2 medium ripe tomatoes and 2 cups of diced pineapple, preferably fresh. Add them to the skillet or wok with the vegetables in the "soft" category. For the sauce, use the Sweet and Sour variation for Basic Chinese Sauce (page 48).

THE LOGICAL VEGETARIAN

G. K. Chesterton (1874–1936) was a prominent English essayist of the late nineteenth and early twentieth century. He was a foe of our vegetarian friend George Bernard Shaw and the two engaged in public and written debate on vegetarianism and other subjects. Chesterton could be quite cantankerous in his anti-vegetarian essays, but in this tongue-in-cheek poem, he was a bit more charming.

You will find me drinking rum,
Like a sailor in a slum,
You will find me drinking beer like a
*   Bavarian.*
You will find me drinking gin
In the lowest kind of inn,
Because I am a rigid Vegetarian.

So I cleared the inn of wine,
And I tried to climb the sign,
And I tried to hail the constable as
*   'Marion'.*
But he said I couldn't speak,
And he bowled me to the Beak
Because I was a Happy Vegetarian.

Oh, I knew a Doctor Gluck,
And his nose it had a hook,
And his attitudes were anything but
*   Aryan;*
So I gave him all the pork
That I had, upon a fork
Because I am myself a Vegetarian.

I am silent in the Club,
I am silent in the pub,
I am silent on a bally peak in Darien;
For I stuff away for life
Shoving peas in with a knife,
Because I am at heart a Vegetarian.

No more the milk of cows
Shall pollute my private house
Than the milk of the wild mares of the
*   Barbarian;*
I will stick to port and sherry,
For they are so very, very,
So very, very, very Vegetarian.

STIR-FRIED VEGETABLES WITH TOFU

This stir-fry is less elaborate than those on the two previous pages, and has more emphasis on the tofu. It is super-quick to make and has the zip of an extra measure of sherry, since Chesterton has assured us that it is so very vegetarian.

2 tablespoons sesame oil
2 medium green peppers, diced
1 large celery stalk, sliced diagonally
2 cloves garlic, minced
1½ cups fresh mung bean sprouts
2 to 3 bunches scallions, chopped
¼ cup toasted sunflower seeds
¼ cup dry sherry
2 to 3 tablespoons soy sauce or tamari
½ teaspoon freshly grated ginger
3 cakes tofu (bean curd), diced
Crisp Chinese noodles for garnish,
**   optional**

Heat the sesame oil in a large skillet or wok. When it is hot, add the green peppers, celery, and garlic, and stir-fry over moderate heat until the peppers and celery are about half done; add the bean sprouts, scallions, and sunflower seeds, and continue to stir-fry just until the bean sprouts are wilted and the remaining vegetables are tender-crisp.

Add the remaining ingredients and lower the heat. Sauté for another 2 or 3 minutes, or until everything is nicely heated through. Serve on its own or over grains or noodles.

4 servings.

LEEK PIE WITH POTATO CRUST

2 medium potatoes, peeled and grated
2 large leeks
2 tablespoons butter
1½ cups sliced mushrooms
4 tablespoons dry white wine
2 eggs, beaten
¼ cup bread crumbs
½ cup ricotta cheese
1 teaspoon dried dill
½ teaspoon dried oregano
¼ teaspoon dry mustard
Pinch of nutmeg
Salt and freshly ground pepper to taste
¼ cup grated Parmesan cheese

Preheat the oven to 375°F (190°C).

Place the grated potatoes in a colander. Let drain for 10 minutes, then squeeze out some of the moisture. Discard all but about 2 inches (5 cm) of the green leaves of the leeks, leaving only the more tender leaves. (You can save the tough leaves for making soup stock.) Slice the leeks into ¼-inch (⅔ cm) rings, then separate them by pushing through the center. Wash carefully, removing all the grit.

Heat the butter in a skillet until it begins to foam. Add the leek rings and sauté over moderately low heat for 5 minutes, stirring frequently. Add the mushrooms and the wine and sauté until the mushrooms are just tender. Transfer to a mixing bowl.

In the same skillet, heat a drop of oil and 2 tablespoons of water and cook the grated potato until nearly tender, but do not brown. Add water as needed to keep it from sticking.

In the meantime, add to the leeks and mushrooms the beaten eggs, bread crumbs, ricotta cheese, and seasonings. When the potatoes are ready, stir the Parmesan cheese into them, and add a little salt and pepper.

Oil a 9-inch (23 cm) round or square baking dish and pat half the potato mixture into the bottom. Pour the entire leek mixture over it, smooth it over, and top with the remaining potatoes. Bake for 35 to 40 minutes, or until the potatoes are golden brown and crusty. Let stand for 5 to 10 minutes, then cut into wedges or squares and serve.

4 to 6 servings.

The leek has long been a national emblem of Wales and has decorated the Welsh military uniform. A Welsh soldier of long ago wrote this verse in praise of the leek:

I like the leeke above all herbs and
*   floures;*
When first we wore the same the field
*   was ours.*
The leeke is white and green, whereby
*   is ment*
That Britaines are both stout and
*   eminent.*
Next to the lion and the unicorne,
The leeke's the fairest emblym that is
*   worne.*

POTATOES

"*Let the sky rain potatoes; let it thunder to the tune of 'Greensleeves'.*"

—William Shakespeare
The Merry Wives of Windsor, (ca. 1599)

The humble potato was originally cultivated by the Indians of Peru. It was carried back to Europe by the Spanish, and like other fruits and vegetables, found its way back to the Americas in the sixteenth century via the British. Sweet potatoes took a similar journey, though it is curious to note that botanically, sweet and white potatoes are unrelated—the white potato is a tuber of the nightshade family, and the sweet potato is a tuber of the morning glory family. The word "potato" is actually a corruption of "batata," the West Indian word for sweet potato.

As we know, the Irish took a particular liking to the potato (although there is really no "Irish" potato), and in days past had various medicinal uses for it. It was believed that a stone boiled with potatoes had the power to heal, and that the water they were boiled in alleviated sprains and aches. Other cultures adopted potato folk-medicine of their own, such as tying a potato to the neck in a stocking to ward off a sore throat, carrying a potato in the pocket to ward off rheumatism, rubbing a potato on the skin to soothe a burn, and much more.

Why an entire chapter on potatoes? Like pasta, they are one of those foods that almost everyone loves; they are quite versatile and are a good vehicle for many types of vegetarian dishes, whether main or side portions. Besides, so much lovely lore and wit exist on the subject to serve up with the recipes, that potatoes simply couldn't be shunted off to a corner of the Vegetables chapter.

WINTER POTATO AND STRING BEAN STEW

Potatoes combined with string beans in an herbed tomato sauce make an exceptionally warming winter stew. If you'd like to have this as a main dish, add some diced tofu.

4 medium potatoes, well scrubbed
2 tablespoons olive oil
1 large onion, chopped
3 cloves garlic, minced
1/2 cup chopped fresh parsley
1 1/2 14-ounce (400g) cans imported plum
**   tomatoes with liquid, chopped**
1/4 cup milk
1 tablespoon minced fresh dill or
**   1 teaspoon dry dill**
1 teaspoon paprika
1/2 teaspoon dried oregano
1/2 teaspoon dill seed or caraway seed
1/4 teaspoon dried thyme
1/4 teaspoon dried rosemary
1/4 teaspoon ground fennel seed
2 heaping cups string beans, cut into
**   1-inch (2 1/2 cm) pieces and steamed**
Salt and freshly ground pepper to taste

Cook the potatoes until tender but still firm. When they are done, dice but don't peel them. Preheat the oven to 375°F (190°C).

Heat the olive oil in a large skillet. When it is hot, add the onion and garlic and sauté over moderately low heat until the onion is golden. Add the parsley, tomatoes, milk, and seasonings and simmer over low heat for 5 minutes.

Combine the potatoes, string beans, and sauce in a large casserole dish and mix together. Cover and bake for 30 to 35 minutes.

6 servings.

MOZZARELLA MASHED POTATO PIE

Mashed potatoes become surprisingly elegant in this very simple casserole which is invariably a hit with guests.

5 to 6 medium potatoes
2 to 3 tablespoons butter
²/₃ cup milk or light cream
Salt and freshly ground pepper to taste
¹/₃ cup bread crumbs or a mixture of wheat germ and bread crumbs
¹/₂ pound (225g) mozzarella cheese, grated
Paprika for topping

Cook or bake the potatoes in their skins until tender. Once they are done, preheat the oven to 350°F (180°C).

When the potatoes are cool enough to handle, peel them and place them in a large mixing bowl. Add the butter, cut into small pieces, and mash the potatoes thoroughly. Stir in the milk and salt and pepper.

Oil a 9-inch (23 cm) round (preferably, although you can use a square one) casserole dish well. Use half of the crumbs to line the bottom and sides of the dish. Pour in half the potato mixture and top with half the grated cheese. Repeat with the remaining potato mixture and cheese. Sprinkle the remaining crumbs over the top, followed by a generous sprinkling of paprika.

Bake for 35 to 40 minutes, or until the top is nicely browned. Allow to stand for 10 minutes, then cut into wedges or squares and serve.

6 servings.

"*What I say is that, if a man really likes potatoes, he must be a pretty decent sort of fellow.*"

—A.A. Milne
Not That It Matters (1920)

According to Sir James Frazer, who wrote The Golden Bough, it was customary for Lithuanian peasants to pull each other's hair at the table before eating the newly harvested potatoes. The meaning of this custom, however, escaped him.

POTATO AND ZUCCHINI SKILLET PIE

So often, potatoes need little seasoning to be delicious. This crisp skillet pie, a variation on the traditional Jewish kugel, is one example.

2 medium potatoes, peeled and grated
1 medium zucchini, grated
1 small onion, grated
3 eggs, lightly beaten
¼ cup matzo meal or bread crumbs
Salt and freshly ground pepper to taste

Combine the grated vegetables in a bowl. Pour in the lightly beaten eggs, the crumbs, and salt and pepper. Mix thoroughly.

As for other skillet pies and fritattas of this sort, I recommend a 9-or 10-inch (23 or 25 cm) Silverstone skillet. Divide the potato mixture in half. Follow the directions on page 180 for "How to Fry and Flip a Skillet Pie or Frittata" using one half of the mixture at a time. Let the pies get really nice and brown. Slice into wedges to serve.

Makes 2 pies, or at least 8 side servings.

POTATO AND LENTIL STEW

The flavors of the potatoes and lentils complement each other nicely in this combination which resembles a warm potato salad. It is hearty enough to serve as a main dish.

4 to 5 medium potatoes, well scrubbed
3/4 cup raw lentils

For the dressing:
1½ cups plain yogurt
1 to 1½ tablespoons Dijon mustard, to taste
1 tablespoon soy sauce or tamari
1 tablespoon red wine vinegar
2 teaspoons dill seed or caraway seed
1 teaspoon paprika
1 teaspoon ground coriander
½ teaspoon ground cumin

2 tablespoons olive oil
1 large onion, chopped
1 medium celery stalk, chopped
2 cloves garlic, minced
1/3 cup chopped fresh parsley
Salt and freshly ground pepper to taste

Cook or bake the potatoes in their skins until tender but still firm. Cook the lentils, following the instructions on page 179, to a tender but firm texture.

Combine the ingredients for the dressing in a small bowl and whisk together. Set aside.

Heat the olive oil in a skillet. When it is hot, add the onion, celery, and garlic and sauté over moderately low heat until the onion is golden. Stir in the parsley, then remove from heat and cover.

When the potatoes are done, dice them but don't peel them and put them in a large casserole. Add the cooked lentils, the onion and celery mixture and the dressing. Add salt and pepper to taste and mix thoroughly.

6 servings.

POTATOES AND EGGPLANT IN GREEN HERB SAUCE

Combine this with Dilled Carrot Croquettes (page 125) and Tabouleh (page 44) for a hearty and attractive meal.

Safflower or vegetable oil
4 to 5 medium potatoes, peeled and thinly sliced
1 medium eggplant, peeled and diced
2 cloves garlic, minced
Wheat germ
1 recipe Green Herb Sauce (page 54)
½ cup sliced or chopped black olives

Heat enough oil to coat the bottom of 2 large, separate skillets. Add to each about ¼ cup water, and place in one the potatoes, and in the other the eggplant and garlic. Cover each and cook over moderately low heat, stirring occasionally, and adding just enough water to keep the bottom of the skillets moist if need be.

The eggplant will be done long before the potatoes. When it is tender, but not mushy, sprinkle in enough wheat germ to coat the pieces evenly. Cover and remove from the heat. At this point, prepare the Green Herb Sauce according to recipe. When it is done, cover and remove from heat. The potatoes should be done shortly thereafter, and should be lightly browned.

Heat the eggplant through as needed, then transfer both it and the potatoes to a large casserole dish. Add the sauce and black olives. Toss together well.

4 to 6 servings.

"*Be eating one potato, peeling a second, have a third in your fist, and your eye on a fourth.***"**

—Old Irish Proverb

Potatoes on the table
  To eat with other things,
Potatoes with their jackets off
  May do for dukes and kings.

But if you wish to taste them
  As nature meant you should,
Be sure to keep their jackets on
  And eat them in a wood.

A little salt and pepper,
  A deal of open air,
And never was a banquet
  That offered nobler fare.

—Edward Verall Lucas (1868–1938)

POTATO BREAD KUGEL

Potato kugel is a traditional Jewish specialty, sometimes fried, and sometimes baked, but always the idea is to get the outside brown and crisp, while leaving the inside soft and moist. In this baked version, bread soaked in milk adds substance to the soft inner texture.

5 medium potatoes, peeled and grated
4 average slices whole grain bread
3/4 cup milk
1 large onion, grated
3 tablespoons safflower or vegetable oil
Salt and freshly ground pepper to taste

Preheat the oven to 375°F (190°C).

Place the grated potatoes in a colander and let drain for 10 minutes. Then squeeze out the moisture.

Tear the bread into small pieces and put in a large mixing bowl. Cover with the milk and allow to soak until the potatoes are ready. Add the grated potatoes, onion, and the remaining ingredients. Mix thoroughly.

Pour into an oiled deep 9-by 9-inch (23 by 23 cm) casserole dish and bake for 50 to 60 minutes, or until the outside is well browned and the potatoes inside are tender.

6 or more servings.

Note: If you grate the potatoes in a food processor, steam or sauté them for a few minutes first, as the processor grates more coarsely than a hand grater, and this would otherwise add to the baking time.

NEW WORLD TZIMMES

Tzimmes, like kugel, is a traditional Jewish specialty. A rich, sweet potato casserole, it symbolizes the sweet things in life at Jewish holiday dinners.

3 large sweet potatoes, well scrubbed
3 tablespoons butter
2 large carrots, sliced
2 medium sweet apples, peeled, cored, and diced
⅔ cup raisins
⅓ cup chopped walnuts or pecans
½ cup milk
½ cup plain yogurt or sour cream
¼ cup honey, more or less to taste
½ teaspoon cinnamon
¼ teaspoon ground cloves
Pinch of nutmeg
1 teaspoon salt

Cook or bake the potatoes in their skins until tender but firm. Once they are done, preheat the oven to 350°F (180°C).

Heat 2 tablespoons of the butter in a skillet until it foams. Add the carrots and sauté over moderately low heat until they are nearly tender. Add the apples and sauté until they soften a bit.

When the sweet potatoes are done, peel them and cut them into fairly large dice and place in a mixing bowl. Combine with the sautéed carrots and apples and the remaining ingredients and mix thoroughly.

Pour into an oiled deep casserole dish, cover, and bake for 20 to 30 minutes.

6 servings.

❝Human nature will not flourish, any more than a potato, if it be planted and replanted, for too long a series of generations, in the same worn out soil.❞

—Nathaniel Hawthorne
The Scarlet Letter (1850)

LES TROIS POMMES

A seventeenth-century writer said of potatoes, "Eating of these roots doth excite Venus and increaseth lust." Serve this sinfully rich, romantic combination of white potato and sweet potato, subtly sweetened with apple, to your honey for favorable results.

4 medium potatoes, well scrubbed
2 medium sweet potatoes, well scrubbed
2 tablespoons butter
1 large onion, chopped
1 large sweet apple, peeled, cored, and
  thinly sliced
¾ cup sour cream
2 cups grated mild white cheese
1 cup light cream
Pinch of nutmeg
Salt to taste

Cook or bake the white and sweet potatoes in their skins until tender but firm. Once they are done, preheat the oven to 350°F (180°C).

Heat the butter in a skillet until it is foamy. Add the onion and sauté over moderately low heat until it is lightly browned.

When the potatoes are cool enough to handle, peel and slice them and put them in a large mixing bowl. Add the sautéed onion and the remaining ingredients and mix thoroughly. Pour into an oiled, large shallow baking dish and bake for 35 minutes.

6 or more servings.

GOLDEN POTATO-CHEESE SQUARES

For a colorful meal, serve this with Tomatoes Stuffed with Curried Eggplant (page 126) and Marinated Broccoli and Cauliflower (page 33).

5 to 6 medium potatoes, well scrubbed
2 tablespoons butter
1 cup milk
2 eggs, separated
2 cups firmly packed grated Cheddar,
  Colby, Edam, or Gouda cheese
2 teaspoons Dijon mustard
1 teaspoon paprika
Salt and freshly ground pepper to taste
½ teaspoon ground turmeric, optional

Cook or bake the potatoes in their skins until tender. Once they are done, preheat the oven to 350°F (180°C).

When the potatoes are cool enough to handle, peel them and put them in a large mixing bowl with the butter, cut into small pieces, and a little of the milk. Mash until smooth.

Add the remaining milk, the egg yolks, and the remaining ingredients and mix thoroughly.

Beat the egg whites until stiff and fold gently into the potato mixture. Oil a large shallow baking casserole and pour the potato mixture into it. Bake for 30 minutes. Allow to stand for 5 to 10 minutes, then cut into squares and serve.

6 or more servings.

"*The greatest cure for a batting slump ever invented.* "

—Babe Ruth (1895–1948)
   on scallions

__ SCALLIONED POTATO BAKE __

If you've been having a batting slump lately, try the Babe's remedy.

5 to 6 medium potatoes, well scrubbed
2 tablespoons butter
1 medium zucchini, sliced
5 to 6 bunches scallions, chopped
3 tablespoons chopped fresh parsley
3/4 cup milk
1/2 cup sour cream or plain yogurt
1 cup grated mild white cheese
1 teaspoon dried dill
Salt and freshly ground pepper to taste
4 hard-boiled eggs, optional
Toasted sunflower seeds for topping

Cook or bake the potatoes in their skins until tender. Once they are done, preheat the oven to 325° (165°C). When the potatoes are cool enough to handle, peel and slice them.

Heat the butter in a skillet until it foams. Add the zucchini, scallions, and parsley, and sauté over moderately low heat just until they have lost their raw quality. Do not brown.

Combine the potatoes, sautéed vegetables, and the remaining ingredients, except the sunflower seeds, in a large mixing bowl and mix together. Pour into an oiled, large shallow baking dish. Sprinkle with the toasted sunflower seeds and bake for 30 to 35 minutes, or until the top is lightly browned.

4 to 6 servings.

In European folk belief, it was said that potatoes should be planted on a starry night so that they'd have many eyes.

POTATO KNISHES

Many cultures have their unique ways of combining potatoes with pastry. On these two pages are three very different possibilities. All take some time to do, but are not difficult. Potato knishes are in the Jewish tradition and rely primarily on the good, basic flavor of the potatoes.

For the potato dough:
2 medium potatoes
1 egg, beaten
1 tablespoon safflower or vegetable oil
2 tablespoons milk
³/₄ cup whole wheat flour
³/₄ cup unbleached white flour
2 teaspoons baking powder
1 teaspoon salt

For the filling:
4 medium potatoes
2 tablespoons melted butter
1 cup milk
Salt and freshly ground pepper to taste

Before starting, have ready 6 potatoes which have been well scrubbed and cooked or baked in their skin until tender.

For the dough, peel the 2 potatoes and mash them well in a mixing bowl. Add to them the beaten egg, oil, and milk and mix well. In a separate bowl, combine the flours, baking powder and salt. Work the mixture into the potato mixture to form a sticky dough. Turn it out onto a well-floured board, and knead for several minutes, adding flour until the dough loses its stickiness. Shape into a ball and cover with a towel.

Preheat the oven to 350°F (180°C).

Peel and mash the 4 remaining potatoes well. Add to them the melted butter, milk, salt and pepper. Mix until smooth.

To assemble the knishes, divide the dough into 4 parts. Roll the dough out into thin sheets, and cut as many 5-inch (13 cm) squares as possible, reusing any dough that has been cut away. Place a bit of the potato mixture in the center of each square, as much as it will hold comfortably, and fold each corner toward the center, overlapping each just a little. Pinch the corners shut. Arrange the knishes on an oiled and floured baking sheet. Bake for 35 minutes, or until the dough is lightly browned.

Makes about 10 knishes.

SAMOSAS

A crisp pastry filled with mildly curried potatoes, Samosas are Indian in origin. Though they are bit of a project to make, they turn a curried dinner into a feast. Very little oil is absorbed by them as they fry.

For the pastry:
³/₄ cup unbleached white flour
³/₄ cup whole wheat flour
¹/₂ teaspoon salt
¹/₃ cup water
3 tablespoons melted butter

Combine the flours and salt in a mixing bowl. Add the water and melted butter and work into a stiff dough. Knead for 3 to 4 minutes, then cover with a towel and let rest while preparing filling.

For the filling:
2 cups diced cooked and peeled potato (about 2 medium)
1 tablespoon butter
¹/₄ cup milk
¹/₂ cup steamed fresh or (thawed) frozen green peas
1¹/₂ teaspoons good curry powder or Home-Mixed Curry (page 170)
¹/₄ teaspoon ground turmeric
¹/₄ teaspoon ground coriander
Salt and freshly ground pepper to taste
Safflower or vegetable oil for frying

Place the diced potato in a mixing bowl. Add the butter and mash well. Add the remaining filling ingredients and mix thoroughly.

Turn the pastry dough out onto a floured board and divide it into 12 balls (about 1 inch, 2¹/₂ cm, in diameter). Flatten each ball and roll it out as thinly and as rounded as possible. Place a small amount of filling on one half of the circle, about ¹/₄ inch (²/₃ cm) from the edge. (You'll discover its capacity after doing one.) Fold the other half over and press the edges closed with the tines of a fork. Turn the samosa over and press the edges on the other side as well.

Heat ¹/₂ inch (1¹/₂ cm) of oil in heavy skillet. When the oil is hot enough to make a drop of water really sizzle, carefully drop in a few of the samosas at a time, and fry on both sides until the pastry is golden brown. Remove with a slotted spoon and drain on paper towels.

Makes 12; about 6 servings.

POTATO AND SPINACH STRUDEL

Inspired by the Greek favorites boreka and spanako-pita, I devised this recipe to include certain elements of both. In most dishes using strudel leaves, or filo, an enormous amount of buttering is required. However, I found that buttering only every third leaf was plenty and the result was just as crisp and delectable.

5 medium potatoes, well scrubbed
³/₄ pound (340g) spinach, stemmed, well washed, and finely chopped, or 1 10-ounce (285g) package frozen chopped spinach, thawed.
1¹/₄ cups buttermilk
¹/₄ teaspoon dried basil
¹/₄ teaspoon dried thyme
Pinch nutmeg
Salt and freshly ground pepper to taste
9 sheets frozen filo (strudel leaves), thawed
¹/₄ cup butter (¹/₂ stick)
¹/₄ pound (115g) feta cheese, finely crumbled

Cook or bake the potatoes in their skins until tender. When cool enough to handle, peel and mash well in a bowl. If you're using fresh spinach, steam it until wilted. Whether fresh or frozen, drain well and add to the mashed potatoes along with the buttermilk and the seasonings. Mix thoroughly. Preheat the oven to 375°F (190°C).

Cut the filo in half so that you have 18, 8¹/₂- by 12-inch (21¹/₂ by 30 cm) leaves. You will need to use a shallow baking dish of approximately this size; if necessary trim the filo to fit. Butter the baking dish well. Melt the remaining butter. Place 3 filo leaves in the baking dish. Use a pastry brush to spread the top one lightly but evenly with butter. Place 3 more leaves in the dish and butter again. Pour in half the potato mixture, spread evenly and sprinkle with half the feta cheese. Repeat the placing and buttering process with the next 6 leaves, then spread the remaining potato mixture over them followed by the remaining feta cheese. Top with the remaining leaves in the same way and pour whatever butter remains over the top and brush it on evenly. Cut into 12 squares and bake for about 45 minutes, or until the top layer of filo looks brown and crisp.

6 servings.

QUICK BREADS AND SWEETS

Each tree
Laden with fairest fruit, that
*   hung to th'eye*
Tempting, stirr'd in me sudden
*   appetite*
To pluck and eat.

—John Milton (1608–1674)
Paradise Lost

Bread, the most basic of foods for many cultures, is in all its simplicity the symbol of plenty. Sacred to many, bread is the object of rituals of the harvest and of religion.

Bread is also associated with home, hearth, and family, and few things evoke such a strong sense of comfort and nostalgia as the scent of freshly baked bread. Unfortunately, most people now have neither the time nor the inclination to bake their own bread, and my busy life, as much as I love home cooking, rarely allows me the hours it takes to prepare yeasted bread doughs for baking. As an alternative, I am offering here several quick bread recipes which can be popped in and out of the oven in a relatively short time. These can at least approximate the pleasure of freshly baked loaves.

"Bread is better than the song of birds."

—Danish Proverb

QUICK BUTTERMILK WHEAT BREAD

It is surprising how very quickly the breads on these two pages can be put together, and how high they rise even without yeast.

1¾ cup whole wheat flour
¾ cup unbleached white flour
¼ cup wheat germ
2½ teaspoons baking powder
1 teaspoon salt
1½ cups buttermilk
¼ cup honey
¼ cup safflower or vegetable oil
1 egg, beaten

Preheat the oven to 350°F (180°C).

Oil and flour a 9-by-5-inch (23 by 13 cm) loaf pan.

Combine the first 5 ingredients in a mixing bowl and stir together.

Stir the buttermilk, honey, and oil into the beaten egg until well blended. Add the wet ingredients to the dry, a little at a time, and mix vigorously until well blended.

Pour into the prepared loaf pan.

Bake for 55 to 60 minutes, or until a knife inserted in the center comes out clean.

Makes 1 loaf.

CHEESE-HERB BREAD

1 cup whole wheat flour
1 cup unbleached white flour
2½ teaspoons baking powder
½ teaspoon salt
½ teaspoon dried basil
½ teaspoon dried dill
¼ teaspoon dried marjoram
¼ teaspoon dried thyme
2 eggs
2 tablespoons honey
½ cup milk
¼ cup safflower or vegetable oil
1¼ cups grated mild Cheddar or Monterey
    Jack cheese

Preheat the oven to 350°F (180°C).

Combine the first 8 ingredients in a large mixing bowl. Stir together until well mixed.

In a separate bowl, beat the eggs, and stir in the honey, milk, and oil until well blended. Add the wet ingredients to the dry, a little at a time. Stir briskly until thoroughly blended. Add the cheese and stir until it is evenly distributed within the dough.

Oil and flour a 9- by 5-inch (23 by 13 cm) loaf pan and transfer the dough into it. Bake for 50 minutes, or until the top is golden brown and a knife inserted in the center comes out clean.

Makes 1 loaf.

" *Without bread, even a palace is sad, but with it a pine tree is paradise.* **"**

—Slavic Proverb

Long ago, it was believed that if cumin was fed to lovers, it would inspire them to remain faithful. It was customary for young ladies in Europe to present their soldier sweethearts with loaves of bread baked with cumin in order to insure their loyalty until their return.

CUMIN CORN KERNEL BREAD

I can't promise you that this bread will keep your loved one faithful, but it will enhance bean dishes very nicely. Serve this with Kidney Bean and Vegetable Chili (page 87).

1 cup cornmeal
¼ cup whole wheat flour
¼ cup unbleached white flour
¼ cup wheat germ
2½ teaspoons baking powder
1 teaspoon salt
1 teaspoon ground cumin
2 eggs, beaten
1 cup milk
2 tablespoons honey
3 tablespoons butter, melted
⅔ cup cooked fresh or (thawed) frozen
    corn kernels

Preheat the oven to 375°F (190°C).

Combine the first 7 ingredients in a mixing bowl.

In a separate bowl, combine the beaten eggs with the remaining ingredients. Slowly add the wet ingredients to the dry until well blended.

Pour into an oiled 9- by 9-inch (23 by 23 cm) baking pan. Bake for 25 to 30 minutes, or until the top is lightly browned and a knife tests clean when inserted into the batter. Cut into squares to serve.

ONION RYE BREAD

Rather than make you weep, this bread will probably make you smile. It goes nicely with hearty soups, such as Lentil and Brown Rice Soup (page 26), when they are going to comprise the main part of your meal.

2 cups rye flour
1/2 cup unbleached white flour
3 tablespoons wheat germ
2 tablespoons brown sugar
1 teaspoon salt
2 1/2 teaspoons baking powder
1 egg, beaten
2/3 cup milk
1/3 cup sour cream
2 tablespoons butter
1 small onion, finely chopped
Lots of caraway or poppy seeds for
**   topping, optional**

Preheat the oven to 350°F (180°C).

Combine the first 6 ingredients in a mixing bowl and stir together.

In a separate bowl, combine the beaten egg with the milk and sour cream and blend. Heat the butter in a small skillet until it begins to foam. Add the onion and sauté over low heat until it is golden, then stir it into the egg-milk mixture.

Add the wet ingredients into the dry, a little at a time, stirring briskly until the ingredients are well blended into a sticky dough.

Oil and flour a 9- by 5-inch (23 by 13 cm) loaf pan and, with the aid of a cake spatula, transfer the dough into it. Bake for 50 to 55 minutes, or until the top is golden and a knife inserted in the center comes out clean.

Makes 1 loaf.

"Onions can make ev'n heirs and widows weep."

—Benjamin Franklin
Poor Richard's Almanack (1734)

ZUCCHINI BREAD

The grated zucchini almost disappears once this rich, cake-like bread is baked, but leaves tiny green specks and a special kind of moistness. This is a good way to use up those mammoth zucchinis of late summer that aren't so good for cooking. If you use that type, discard the seedy pulp.

3 eggs, well beaten
3/4 cup safflower or vegetable oil
2/3 cup brown sugar
2/3 cup white sugar
2 teaspoons vanilla extract
2 cups coarsely grated, peeled zucchini
2 1/2 cups unbleached white flour
1/2 cup wheat germ
3 teaspoons baking powder
1 teaspoon salt
1 teaspoon baking soda
1 teaspoon cinnamon
1/2 teaspoon ground cloves
3/4 cup chopped walnuts

Preheat the oven to 350°F (180°C).

In a large mixing bowl, blend the beaten eggs with the oil, sugars, and vanilla. Stir in the grated zucchini, then add the flour, half at a time, mixing it in after each addition.

Add the remaining ingredients and mix thoroughly.

Pour into 2 oiled and floured 9- by 5-inch (23 by 13 cm) loaf pans and bake for 45 to 50 minutes, or until nicely browned and a knife inserted in the center comes out clean.

Makes 2 loaves.

Shaw, as mentioned in the introduction, was a vegetarian for nearly seventy years, and really did relish good food. It was well known, however, that he had quite a sweet tooth and ate massive quantities of cakes, pastries, and honey. He managed to stay ever slender and lived to be ninety-four. In moderation, an occasional treat does not hurt.

In all the sweets that follow are included some healthy elements such as fruits, nuts, wheat germ, and other whole grain substances, and dairy products.

BROWN RICE PUDDING

William Vaughn in Directions for Health *(1600), said "Rice sodden with milk and sugar qualifieth wonderfully the heat of the stomake, increaseth genital seede, and stoppeth the flux of the belly." I don't know if these claims are entirely true, but rice pudding does seem comforting, and children seem especially to like it.*

1½ cups raw brown rice
1 egg, well beaten
⅓ cup honey, more or less to taste
1 medium sweet apple, peeled, cored, and coarsely grated
¾ cup raisins
1 cup light cream
2 teaspoons vanilla extract
1 teaspoon cinnamon
¼ teaspoon nutmeg
¼ teaspoon ground cloves

Cook the rice as directed in Cooking Grains (page 178). Once it is done, preheat the oven to 325°F (165°C).

Combine the cooked rice in a mixing bowl with the remaining ingredients. Mix thoroughly, and pour the mixture into an oiled, large shallow baking dish. Cover and bake for 30 minutes. Then uncover and bake for 5 minutes longer.

8 or more servings.

"There is no love sincerer than the love of food. "

—George Bernard Shaw
Man and Superman (1903)

APPLE CRISP

This version of old-fashioned Apple Crisp, a very easy and healthy dessert, was given to me by a friend who assured me that it's even better served warm over vanilla ice cream—she was right.

4 or 5 medium sweet apples, peeled and sliced
1/3 cup chopped walnuts or pecans
1/2 teaspoon cinnamon
1/4 teaspoon ground cloves

For the topping:
3 tablespoons butter, somewhat softened
1/4 cup whole wheat flour
2 to 3 tablespoons brown sugar, to taste
3 tablespoons wheat germ
1/4 teaspoon cinnamon
1/4 teaspoon nutmeg

Preheat the oven to 350°F (180°C).

Combine the first 4 ingredients in a mixing bowl, and mix together until the spices coat the apples more or less evenly. Butter an 8- by 8-inch (20 by 20 cm) or 9- by 9-inch (23 by 23 cm) baking pan and arrange the apples in it.

Cut the butter into thin slices and place in a mixing bowl. Add the remaining topping ingredients and cream together with a fork until a crumbly mixture is formed. Sprinkle evenly over the apples and bake for 50 to 60 minutes, or until the apples are done and the crust is browned.

Serve on its own or over vanilla ice cream.

4 to 6 servings.

OF APPLES AND GRAVITY

The apple has been the subject of legend and proverb, in the guise of a love charm, a magical object, and a cure for every ill. But nowhere did the apple have such practical application as in the true story of Isaac Newton's formulation of the theory of gravity. In 1666, while having tea, Newton observed the falling of an apple in his garden. It was this event that led him to the concept of universal force, which is to say, that although the falling of an apple from a tree seems different than the orbiting of the moon, the moon is in fact constantly falling toward the earth in much the same way. The earth's gravity pulling on the moon keeps it from flying off its orbit. Think of this the next time you have apple pie or gaze at the moon.

"...It has been shown as proof-positive that carefully prepared chocolate is as healthful a food as it is pleasant; that it is nourishing and easily digested; that it does not cause the same harmful effects to feminine beauty which are blamed on coffee but is on the contrary a remedy for them; that it is above all helpful to people who must do a great deal of mental work, to those who labor in the pulpit or in the classroom, and especially to travellers..."

—Jean Anthelme Brillat-Savarin
The Physiology of Taste (1825)

CHOCOLATE CHIP PEANUT CAKE

Now that chocolate has the endorsement of the famous gastronome Brillat-Savarin, let's get to it! Semisweet chocolate chips are my favorite way to indulge, so here are presented two sinfully delicious ways to enjoy them.

1/4 cup (1/2 stick) butter, softened
1/2 cup peanut butter
1/3 cup brown sugar
1 egg, beaten
1/2 cup milk
3/4 cup whole wheat flour
1 1/2 teaspoons baking powder
1/2 teaspoon salt
1/3 cup chopped peanuts
6 ounces (180g) semisweet chocolate
    chips

Preheat the oven to 375°F (190°C).

Cream together the butter, peanut butter, and brown sugar. Add the beaten egg and milk and stir until well blended. Stir in the flour, a little at a time, then add the remaining ingredients. Stir together until thoroughly blended. Pour into an oiled 8- by 8-inch (20 by 20 cm) or 9- by 9-inch (23 by 23 cm) square cake pan. Bake for 25 to 30 minutes, or until the top is golden brown. Allow to cool and cut into squares to serve.

CHOCOLATE COVERED WINTER FRUIT PIE

Eating this pie produces the curious sensation that one is having something very healthy yet very sinful at the same time.

1 large, sweet apple, peeled, cored and
    thinly sliced
1 medium orange, sectioned and chopped
1 medium banana, sliced
1 medium pear, thinly sliced
1/4 cup Amaretto or Grand Marnier
1/4 cup chopped dates or black figs
1 teaspoon cinnamon
1/4 teaspoon ground cloves
1/4 teaspoon ground fennel seed, optional
1 regular, unbaked 9-inch (23 cm) pie shell
6 ounces (180g) semisweet chocolate
    chips
3/4 cup rolled oats
1/4 cup wheat germ
3 tablespoons melted butter

Preheat the oven to 350°F (180°C).

Combine the fruits in a mixing bowl with the liqueur, dried fruit, and spices. Mix well. Transfer the mixture to the pie shell and top as evenly as possible with the chocolate chips, making sure to get them into the crevices around the edges as well.

Combine the oats and wheat germ in a small bowl. Pour the melted butter over the oats and wheat germ and stir until they are evenly coated. Sprinkle the mixture evenly over the top of the pie.

Bake for 50 minutes, or until the oats are lightly browned, the fruit is done, and the chocolate chips are melted. This pie is best served warm.

SESAME-DATE BROWNIES

Sesame seeds are reported by the Kama Sutra to have definite aphrodisiac effects. One concoction listed results in a confection enabling a man to "enjoy innumerable women." I wouldn't make that claim for this sesame, date and nut treat, but I will say that it makes a high-energy snack.

¼ cup dry, unsweetened cocoa
½ to ⅔ cup brown sugar, to taste
½ cup whole wheat flour
¼ cup unbleached white flour
⅔ cup sesame seeds
1 teaspoon baking powder
½ teaspoon salt
2 eggs
¼ cup milk
¼ cup (½ stick) butter, melted
1½ cups pitted dates, finely chopped
¼ cup almonds or walnuts, finely chopped

Preheat oven to 350°F (180°C).

Combine the first 7 ingredients in a mixing bowl and stir together until well blended.

Beat the eggs and milk well in a separate bowl. Stir the melted butter into the egg-milk mixture. Add the wet ingredients to the dry, a little at a time, and stir briskly until thoroughly blended.

Combine the chopped dates and nuts.

Oil a shallow baking pan approximately 8- by 14-inch (20 by 35 cm) and pour half the batter into it. Spread the date-nut mixture over it as evenly as possible, then top with the remaining batter. Bake for 25 to 30 minutes, or until a knife inserted into the center comes out clean. Allow to cool and cut into squares to serve.

FRESH PEACH CRUMB CAKE

Sweet but firm peaches are best for this cake.

1 cup wheat germ
³/₄ cup unbleached white flour
¹/₃ cup brown sugar
1 teaspoon cinnamon
¹/₂ teaspoon nutmeg
¹/₄ teaspoon powdered ginger
¹/₄ cup (¹/₂ stick) butter, melted
3 heaping cups thin peach slices (about 3 large peaches, or 4 to 5 smaller ones)
²/₃ cup chopped almonds
¹/₃ cup milk

Preheat the oven to 325°F (165°C).

Combine the first 6 ingredients in a mixing bowl. Combine the butter with the dry ingredients until they are evenly coated and have a crumb-like texture.

Oil a 9-inch (23 cm) round or square cake pan. Spread one third of the crumbs over the bottom. Arrange half of the peach slices in overlapping rows over the crumbs, then sprinkle half of the almonds and half of the milk over them. Repeat with another third of the crumbs, the remaining peaches, almonds, and milk, and finally the remaining crumbs. Cover and bake for 20 minutes, then uncover and bake for 20 minutes longer. Cool before serving.

> **"***Better one bite of the peach of immortality than a whole basket of apricots.***"**
>
> —Chinese Proverb

This is a depiction after a Chinese sculpture in wood of Shou-Lao, the God of long life. Shou-Lao holds a peach, which is in Chinese tradition the symbol of longevity and immortality. In Taoist depictions of immortality, an old man emerges from a peach. The peach is also a feminine sexual symbol in the Orient, and its blossoms are the emblem of a bride.

> **"**_The use of Honey is so soveraigne that nothing in our cold countries comes neare it for goodnesse and perfection: insomuch that it is rightly called Flos Florum, the flower of flowers, or rather their quintessence. It makes old men young, preserving their naturall heate, if they know how to use it._ **,,**

—William Vaughn
  Directions for Health (1617)

HONEYED SWEET POTATO PIE

Sweet potato pie originates from the American south. Making it with honey rather than sugar enhances the velvety smooth texture even more. This is often mistaken for pumpkin pie, so similar is the flavor and texture.

2 heaping cups firmly packed cooked diced sweet potato (about 1 very large sweet potato)
1 egg
½ cup milk
1 teaspoon vanilla or almond extract
⅓ cup honey, more or less to taste
1 teaspoon cinnamon
½ teaspoon nutmeg
¼ teaspoon ground cloves
1 teaspoon dry unsweetened cocoa
1 regular, unbaked 9-inch (23 cm) pie shell

Preheat the oven to 350°F (180°C).

Put the diced potato into the workbowl of a food processor or blender. Add the remaining ingredients and process until completely smooth. Pour into the pie shell.

Bake for 50 minutes. Allow to cool before serving.

FRESH STRAWBERRY-CITRUS CUSTARD CAKE

A thin, baked batter serves as an anchor for a fresh citrus custard full of fresh strawberries.

For the batter:
1/2 cup whole wheat flour
1/2 cup unbleached white flour
1 1/2 teaspoons baking powder
1/4 teaspoon salt
1 egg, well beaten
3 tablespoons honey
3 tablespoons melted butter
1/3 cup milk
Juice of 1/2 lemon

Preheat the oven to 375°F (190°C).

Combine the first 4 ingredients in a mixing bowl. Then, combine the remaining ingredients in another bowl and mix until well blended. Stir into the dry ingredients until well mixed. Oil a 9-inch (23 cm) round or square baking pan and pour the batter into it. Bake for 20 to 25 minutes, or until lightly browned.

Start on the custard once the batter is out of the oven.

For the custard:
1/2 cup fresh-squeezed orange juice
Juice of 1 lemon
Grated rind of 1/2 lemon
2 to 3 tablespoons honey, to taste
2 eggs, beaten
2 tablespoons Amaretto or Grand Marnier, optional
1 tablespoon cornstarch
1 pint strawberries, hulled and quartered

Put all the ingredients, except the strawberries, in a heavy saucepan. (Dissolve the cornstarch in a little water before adding it.) Whisk together as thoroughly as possible and then heat slowly over low heat, whisking continuously for 3 to 4 minutes, or until quite thick. Remove from heat. Stir in the quartered strawberries, and pour the whole mixture over the baked batter. Chill before serving. This is good served either chilled or at room temperature.

UNBAKED CHERRY-CHEESE PIE

With all due respect to Josh Billings, any fresh berry may be substituted to top the pie, such as strawberries (halved), blueberries, raspberries, etc. Since this is unbaked, it makes an ideal summer dessert for special occasions.

For the crust:
1 1/2 cups natural bran flakes
1/2 cup wheat germ
1/2 teaspoon cinnamon
1 tablespoon honey
3 tablespoons melted butter

For the filling:
8 ounces (225g) cream cheese, softened
1/2 cup cottage cheese
2 tablespoons lemon juice
1 teaspoon grated lemon rind
1/4 cup honey
1 egg yolk

For the topping:
1/2 pound (225g) fresh cherries, pitted and halved
1 to 2 tablespoons Amaretto, optional

Crush the bran flakes as finely as possible, either with a rolling pin or in a food processor or blender. Combine them in a small bowl with the remaining crust ingredients, mixing with a fork to distribute the honey and butter. Transfer to a lightly oiled, 9-inch (23 cm) round or square baking pan and pat in well.

Cut the cream cheese into several smaller pieces and put it in the workbowl of a food processor or blender along with the remaining filling ingredients. Process until completely smooth. Pour over the crumb crust and with the aid of a cake spatula, smooth it in evenly. Arrange the cherries on top, cut side down, then drizzle with the Amaretto. Cover and chill for at least 2 hours before serving. Cut into wedges or squares to serve.

> **"Cherrys are good, but they are too mutch like sucking a marble with a handle tew it."**
>
> —Josh Billings
> *His Works, Complete* (1876)

Walnuts were served at wedding feasts in ancient Greece and Rome, where they were regarded as favorable to the fertility of the bridal couple. Conversely, in old Rumania, a bride would place in her bodice one roasted walnut for each year she wished to remain childless.

WALNUT AND MAPLE BAKED PEARS

Like Apple Crisp, this easy fruit and nut dessert is wonderful served over vanilla ice cream.

5 medium pears, preferably the yellow-skinned type (such as bosc)
2 tablespoons butter
1 cup chopped walnuts
⅓ cup natural maple syrup
¼ cup currants or raisins
¼ cup wheat germ
¼ cup milk or light cream
3 tablespoons Amaretto
1 teaspoon vanilla or almond extract
½ teaspoon cinnamon

Preheat the oven to 350°F (180°C).

Cut the pears into quarters lengthwise (you don't have to peel them), remove the cores and stem ends, then cut each quarter in half, lengthwise. Oil a large shallow baking dish and arrange the pear slices in rows, alternating the thin and thick ends so that more slices can fit. Make only a single layer of pears; if you run out of room, use another baking dish.

In a small, heavy saucepan, melt the butter over low heat. Remove from the heat and add to it all the remaining ingredients. Mix thoroughly. Spread the mixture evenly over the pears and bake for 50 minutes. As suggested above, serve warm over vanilla ice cream.

4 to 6 servings.

ALMOND PRESERVE BARS

In keeping with the almond tree's reputation for haste, this dessert can be whipped up very quickly. These are somewhat like cookies; each bar goes a long way.

½ cup whole wheat flour
¼ cup wheat germ
¼ cup brown sugar
2 teaspoons dry, unsweetened cocoa
3 tablespoons melted butter
2 eggs, well beaten
1½ cups finely chopped almonds
**½ cup good quality berry preserves, such
    as blueberry, raspberry, etc.**
1 teaspoon vanilla or almond extract

Preheat oven to 350°F (180°C).

Combine the first 4 ingredients in a small bowl and stir together. Pour the melted butter over the dry ingredients and mix together until they are coated. Set aside.

Combine the beaten eggs with the almonds, preserves, and vanilla. Stir until thoroughly mixed.

Oil an 8- by 8-inch (20 by 20 cm) or 9- by 9-inch (23 by 23 cm) square baking pan. Line the bottom with three quarters of the crumbs mixture and pat it in firmly. Pour over it the almond and preserve mixture, pat in well, and sprinkle the top with the remaining crumbs. Bake for 30 to 35 minutes. Allow to cool and cut into approximately 1- by 2-inch (2½ by 5 cm) bars.

The Hebrew word for almond, "shakad," means to awaken early or to make haste. This name is given to the tree and its fruit due to its rapid growth, and thus, in the ancient Hebrew era the almond tree symbolized haste, as it did in the biblical story of Aaron's rod. Its sudden blossoming was a harbinger of spring.

The Fruit of Knowledge, offered to Eve and Adam in the Garden of Eden, is commonly thought to have been an apple, but the fact is that the apple was never specifically named as such in the Bible. John Gerarde, in his Herball (1636), called the banana tree Adam's Apple Tree, and many Christians and Jews of his time considered the banana tree the Tree of Knowledge.

The fig tree, whose fruit is supposed among the first cultivated by man, was the retreat that Adam found after having eaten of the forbidden fruit. From there he plucked the fig leaf that hid his nakedness, and today, the fig leaf is still an emblem of modesty.

FRUITS OF PARADISE IN CREAM

A friend introduced me to the concept of combining bananas and black figs in cream, and thought that the origin of this dish may be Moroccan. Although I couldn't verify this, I liked the idea and proceeded to embellish it. The result is a rich, spiced winter fruit salad. Look for black figs in imported food shops. They are softer and sweeter than brown figs and are sometimes called mission figs.

2 large bananas, sliced
8 to 10 dried black figs, chopped
1 medium tart apple, peeled, cored, and
    sliced
1/3 cup chopped walnuts, almonds, or
    pecans
1/2 cup heavy cream
1/2 teaspoon vanilla or almond extract
1/2 teaspoon cinnamon
1/4 teaspoon ground cloves
1/4 teaspoon ground cardamom, optional

Combine the first 4 ingredients in a serving bowl. In a small bowl, combine the cream with the remaining ingredients and stir together. Pour over the fruit mixture and mix thoroughly.
    4 servings.

BANANA RAITA

A yogurt-based salad with Indian origins, this, like Cucumber Raita (page 38), is most welcome as a palate-cooler when served with curried dishes. This may be served along with the curries in addition to the Cucumber Raita as an interesting flavor complement, or immediately following, as a post-dinner, pre-dessert refresher.

2 large bananas, sliced
1 cup plain yogurt
1 tablespoon honey
½ teaspoon cinnamon
¼ teaspoon nutmeg
¼ teaspoon ground cardamom, optional
1 to 2 tablespoons chopped fresh mint
       leaves, optional

Combine all the ingredients in a mixing bowl, mix thoroughly, and chill.

4 to 6 servings.

TREATISE ON WHY BANANA AND NOT APPLE WAS INDEED • The Fruit of Knowledge •

The next time you happen upon an area with authentic colonial homes, look for a carving of a pineapple on the doorway or gatepost. The practice of carving or painting pineapples on entrances originated with the Indians of the West Indies, who cultivated the fruit and considered it as a symbol of friendship and hospitality. This custom was taken back to Europe by the Spanish, who spread it to England; it was carried back to the new American colonies. The pineapple symbol was meant to assure visitors that they would receive a warm welcome.

PINEAPPLE AND ORANGES IN YOGURT

This refreshing fruit salad makes for a particularly sweet finish to a Chinese-style feast. If you'd like, serve it with almond cookies.

3 heaping cups diced pineapple, preferably fresh
2 medium oranges, sectioned and seeded
1 cup plain yogurt
½ cup chopped almonds
2 to 3 tablespoons honey, to taste
½ cup shredded coconut
1 tablespoon lemon juice
½ teaspoon anise seed, optional

If fresh pineapple is unavailable and you'd like to use canned, make sure it is unsweetened. Drain it and reserve the juice for another purpose, perhaps to add to a fruit juice.

Combine all the ingredients in a serving bowl and chill before serving.

6 servings.

Nose, nose, jolly red nose,
And what gave thee that jolly red
    nose?
Nutmeg and ginger, cinnamon and
    cloves,
That's what gave me this jolly red
    nose.

—Thomas Ravencroft
Deuteromelia (1609)

SPICY SUMMER FRUIT

The man in this old English rhyme of "nutmeg and ginger, cinnamon and cloves," would have us believe that these spices (not his drinking) caused his red nose. A light touch of these spices nicely enhances this ambrosial fruit salad, which definitely does not cause red noses.

6 to 7 cups fresh summer fruit (choose several from among strawberries, cherries, blueberries, melons, peaches, plums, nectarines, mangoes, etc.), chopped
1½ cups plain yogurt
½ cup chopped almonds, pecans, or walnuts
⅓ cup currants or raisins
2 tablespoons honey
½ teaspoon freshly grated ginger
1 teaspoon cinnamon
¼ teaspoon nutmeg
¼ teaspoon ground cloves

Combine all the ingredients in a large mixing bowl and mix thoroughly. Chill before serving.
6 servings.

HERBS
AND
SPICES

Can you make me a cambric shirt,
Parsley, sage, rosemary, and
    thyme,
Without any seam or needlework?
And you shall be a true lover of
    mine.

Can you wash it in yonder well,
Parsley, sage, rosemary, and
    thyme,
Where never sprung water, not
    rain ever fell?
And you shall be a true lover of
    mine.

Can you dry it on yonder thorn,
Parsley, sage, rosemary, and
    thyme,
Which never bore blossom since
    Adam was born?
And you shall be a true lover of
    mine...

—Old English Song

Herbs and spices once played a much more important role in everyday life than they do today, as they were valued not only for their usefulness on cookery, but for their lovely scent, their beauty as plants, and their medicinal properties. They have been cultivated and used for thousands of years, as far back as ancient India and China and classical Greece and Rome.

As objects of mystery and beauty, herbs and spices have adorned countless poetic lines, with names like elecampane, lavender, lovage, and Angelica. They were also imbued with magical powers, both good and bad. The refrain "parsley, sage, rosemary, and thyme" having been recently made familiar, is actually hundreds of years old, and it is theorized that it was perhaps a witches' incantation, as those herbs were thought to have numerous magical and medicinal properties. Until relatively recently, herbs were the mainstays of everyday medicine, and today, with the superstition sifted out, it is known that they truly do possess wonderful curative values. The Chinese, in fact, have learned to incorporate herbal healing with modern medical technique.

Since vegetarian cookery draws upon such a wide scope of sources, it is useful to know about the culinary herbs and spices. This chapter will serve as a brief overview of those used in the recipes in this book, with a description of their use as it applies in particular to vegetarian cookery, along with a taste of poetry, prose, and lore that has accompanied them through the ages. For those who are curious to know more about this intriguing subject, old herbals can be found in some libraries, and many fine books are in print.

ANISEEDS are the seeds of an herbaceous plant and have a distinctive, pleasant licorice taste and are used to produce the liqueurs anisette, ouzo, and pernod. Anise is most commonly used in baking and gives an unusual twist to fruit desserts (see Pineapple and Oranges in Yogurt, page 164).

In folk belief, sprigs of anise were attached to pillows to ward off unpleasant dreams, and the seeds were eaten in hopes of restoring a youthful appearance to facial features.

BASIL, sometimes called sweet basil, has a history more controversial than that of any herb. Basil is most delightful used fresh, either as a windowsill herb or bought in large, fragrant bunches in late summer and early autumn. If you have an opportunity to use fresh basil, substitute it in a 3 to 1 ratio to dry amounts given in the recipes. Basil has a special affinity for tomato-based dishes and pastas, but fresh or dried, its pleasant fragrance and distinctive flavor also enhance many types of vegetables, grain dishes, salads, and soups.

An herb with many contradictory facets, the origin of its name, basilisk, has meant either "kingly" or a deadly dragon. In the Pasta chapter, basil's association with love in Italy was depicted, as well as the strange way it was sown in ancient Greece (pages 108 and 109), where it was at one time the symbol for hatred. In India, on the other hand, basil was considered a most sacred herb. Basil played an important role in the gory tales of Salome, and later in Isabella and her Pot of Basil. Strangest of all was its unfortunate association with scorpions. It was believed to have been responsible for breeding scorpions both where it grew and in the brain. Paradoxically, basil was also considered an antidote to the scorpion's venom.

Madonna, wherefore hast thou sent to me
Sweet basil and mignonette?
Embleming love and health which never yet
In the same wreath might be.

—Percy Bysshe Shelley (1792–1822)
"To Emiliana Viviani"

168

BAY LEAVES are the leaves of the bay laurel tree. They are used mainly for flavoring soups, stews, and pilafs.

In Greek mythology, the wood-nymph Daphne was so repelled by Apollo's pursuit of her, that she prayed fervently to the gods for protection. They heard her pleas and changed her into a bay laurel tree. Apollo then declared that the laurel tree would remain forever green, and its leaves would henceforth be symbolic of bravery and accomplishment. Laurel leaves were woven into the head wreaths of worthy ancients of Greece and Rome and thus we get the expression "to rest on one's laurels."

The bay laurel tree was once widely believed to have vast supernatural powers:

> **"It is a tree of the Sun, and under the Celestial sign Leo, and resisteth Witchcraft potently, as also all the evils old Saturn can do the body of man...neither witch nor devil, thunder nor lightning, will hurt a man where a bay tree is."**

—Nicolas Culpeper

CARAWAY SEEDS are the seeds of a biennial herb native to Europe. We know them best from their use in rye bread, but they are also good used subtly in potato and cheese dishes.

> **"Nay, you shall see my orchard where in an arbour, we will eat a last year's pippin of mine own grafting, with a dish of carraways, and so forth..."**

—William Shakespeare
Henry IV (ca. 1597)

CARDAMOM refers to the whole or ground aromatic seeds of the fruit of a tall herbal plant that is grown primarily in India and Ceylon. The fruits are pale green pods which contain a dozen or so tiny dark seeds. Used extensively in Indian and other East Asian cookery, cardamom is not widely used in the United States. Aside from its use in curries (see Lusty Curried Peas, page 94) and chutneys, cardamom can be used in ground form for baking; it also goes nicely with bananas (see Banana Raita, page 163), apples, and sweet potato.

CAYENNE PEPPER comes from the ground dried fruit of the capsicum pepper, a climbing plant. It is a very hot spice, useful in curries, chutneys, chilis, cheese dishes, "hot and spicy" Chinese dishes, in fact anywhere that some fire is desired! Until you are well acquainted with its strength, use it sparingly.

> **"Powder thereof put in the nose causeth to snese and clense the brayn of flewmatyke humours as snyvell and rewme."**

—Grete Herball (1529)

CHIVES, see Onion

CILANTRO, see Coriander

CINNAMON comes from the dried, aromatic inner bark of a small evergreen tree. It is one of the oldest spices known, mentioned in ancient Chinese writings and in the Bible. Cinnamon is the most widely used baking spice, and enhances any fresh or baked fruit desserts. It is also very good in curries.

> **"*Cinnamon corroborateth all the powers of the body, restoreth them that bee decayed, purgeth the head, and succoureth the cough.* ,,**
>
> —William Vaughn
> *Directions for Health* (1600)

CLOVES are the dried flower buds of the evergreen clove tree, being most commonly used in ground form for baking. Cloves especially enhance apple and banana desserts and may also be used in curries and chutneys.

The word "clove" comes from the Latin "clavus," meaning nail, as that is what the clove bud resembles.

CORIANDER is the seed of an herbal plant, whose leaves are known as *cilantro*. The seeds are usually used ground and are a most useful spice, with a unique flavor and aromatic quality. They enhance bean and corn dishes, curries, chilies, and soups. The coriander leaves, or cilantro, are sometimes called Spanish or Chinese parsley, and are used in Spanish, Mexican, Chinese, and Indian cookery. The seeds and leaves have an entirely different flavor, and cannot be used interchangeably. If fresh cilantro is unavailable, use fresh Italian parsley, though there is no comparison in flavor.

In the Bible, the food of heaven, Manna, was compared to coriander seed. It was mentioned as an aphrodisiac in *The Thousand and One Nights*, and was one of the plants in the Hanging Gardens of Babylon.

CUMIN comes from the seed-like fruit of a small herb native to the Mediterranean. Although the flavors of coriander and cumin are quite different from one another, they enhance each other wonderfully and I recommend cumin for the same dishes mentioned for coriander. Its spicy yet not overly hot flavor is the basis for premixed curry and chili powders.

Cumin suffered from a bad reputation for a time in ancient Greece, where it symbolized avarice and meanness. Later, however, it was considered to have properties which would cause lovers to remain faithful (see Cumin Corn Kernel Bread, page 150), Pliny the Elder being one of those who advocated it as such.

CURRY, or more specifically, "curry powder" is not a spice in and of itself, but a mixture of several different spices. In true Indian cookery most of these spices are bought whole, toasted, and then ground with a mortar and pestle. A good compromise between this and using commercial curry powder is to mix a batch of good quality, preground spices and store the mixture in a tightly capped jar. A curry mix can have any amount of spices, and result in different types of flavors. Here is a formula that I enjoy using:

HOME-MIXED CURRY
2 teaspoons ground cumin
2 teaspoons ground coriander
2 teaspoons ground turmeric
1 teaspoon nutmeg
1 teaspoon salt
½ teaspoon cinnamon
¼ teaspoon cayenne pepper
**¼ teaspoon freshly ground
  black pepper**

Simply spoon each of the spices into a spice jar and shake well to mix. Compare the rich scent of this mixture with a supermarket curry powder and you won't believe the difference. Another alternative is to buy a pre-mixed curry from a spice shop or an Indian food shop. This is what is referred to in the recipes as "good curry powder."

DILL, sometimes called dill weed, and **DILL SEED** come from a tall, feathery annual plant. Believed to have a soothing effect on both the digestive tract and the mind, the word comes from the Norwegian "dilla," meaning "to lull." The leaves are common both in fresh and dry form and widely useful in soups, salads, dressings, potato and vegetable dishes, and wherever a mixture of herbs is called for. The seeds are used for pickling and are worth experimenting with for the same usages as the leaves, where they have a similar but much subtler effect than caraway seeds. Dill makes a fine windowsill herb.

The herbalist Culpeper said of dill, "Mercury hath dominion of this plant, and therefore to be sure it strengthens the brain." A seventeenth-century physician most charmingly recommended dill to stop "yeox, hicket, hisquet, or hickock," known today as hiccups. Dill was once widely used as a foil against witchcraft:

> **"Trefoil, vervain, John's wort, dill, Hinders witches of their will... "**
>
> —Sir Walter Scott (1771–1832)
> "The Nativity Chant"

FENNEL SEED is the ground seeds of another tall, feathery plant, different from the celery-like variety of fennel that is eaten as a vegetable. Fennel seed is aromatic and has a licorice flavor similar to but subtler than anise. It can be used for baking, fruit desserts, and in small amounts where a mixture of herbs is called for to give an unusual twist (see Winter Potato and String Bean Stew, page 136).

Although no longer a very widely used kitchen spice, fennel seed has a full and fascinating legacy. Pliny the Elder, among others, believed that serpents ate fennel when they shed their skin, in order to renew their youth and strengthen their sight. In Italy, fennel was the symbol of flattery; the expression "dare finnocio," to flatter, literally means "to give fennel." Fennel's virtues were considered so numerous that a thirteenth-century physician said that "he who sees fennel and gathers it not, is not a man but a devil."

> *Above the lowly plants it towers*
> *The fennel, with its yellow flowers,*
> *And in an earlier age than ours,*
> *Was gifted with the wondrous*
>   *powers,*
> *Lost vision to restore...*
>
> —Henry Wadsworth Longfellow (1807–1882)
> "The Goblet of Life"

GARLIC, see Onion

GINGER is the underground stem, or root, of a tropical plant which originated in some Pacific islands. An ancient spice, it was known to Confucius and mentioned in the Koran. Powdered ginger is acceptable for baking, but the freshly grated root is superior for giving Indian and Chinese style cookery an authentic character. It is also pleasant used subtly in fruit salads. Look for ginger root in Oriental groceries, produce markets, and even some supermarkets. Depending on the quantity used, ginger lends anything from a nice zest to fiery heat. Use it conservatively until you know its strength.

> **"Yes, by Saint Anne, the Ginger shall be hot i' thy mouth too. "**
>
> —William Shakespeare
> *Twelfth Night* (ca. 1601)

MARJORAM and **OREGANO** come from small herbaceous plants that are so closely related to one another that they share a botanical name, "origanum," which means in its original Latin, "joy of the mountain." Marjoram is a bit milder than oregano, although a bit more peppery, and they are widely useful for basically the same things: tomato-based dishes that are Italian-style, pastas, salads, vegetables, soups, grain dishes, chilis, and wherever a mixture of herbs is called for.

In legend and poetry, oregano takes a back seat to marjoram. Culpeper's Herbal says that marjoram is warming and comforting, and Gerarde in his Herball claims that it is "good for those who are given to overmuch sighing."

And tho' sweet marjoram will your
*   garden paint*
With no gay colours, yet preserve the
*   plant,*
Whose fragrance will invite your
*   kind regard,*
When her known virtues have her
*   worth declared.*

—Anonymous

MINT is the name for a related variety of plants with aromatic foliage. Spearmint and peppermint are the primary mints used not only for cookery but for mint teas. Mint gives a light, refreshing flavor to certain fruit desserts, raitas (the palate-cooling salads served with curries—see Cucumber Raita, page 38, and Banana Raita, page 163), and has a nice affinity with green peas. Mint is often called for in the classic Tabouleh salad (page 44).

Mint gets its name from a nymph of classical mythology who was called Mintha, or sometimes Minthes. Pluto was in love with her, so his jealous wife turned her into a mint plant.

I am that flower
*   That Mint*
*   That Columbine.*

—William Shakespeare
Love's Labour Lost (ca. 1594)

MUSTARD comes from the seed of an Old World annual. It is useful wherever a subtle hotness is required, whether in soups, cheese dishes, egg dishes, grains, chilis, and curries. Prepared mustard is also made from mustard seed. I recommend the brown, Dijon-style mustard for cookery, and it doesn't have to be terribly expensive to be good.

One of the many legends about mustard relates that Alexander the Great was sent a sack of sesame seeds by Darius of Persia, to show him how vast was the Persian army. Alexander the Great then sent back to Darius a sack of mustard seed, symbolizing not only the size of his army, but its might. A tale from the Orient describes how the Buddha tells a distressed mother who seeks his help that he can bring her dead child to life only if she brings him some mustard seed from a home where no person has died. After an exhaustive search, she realizes that no family is exempt from the experience of death.

NUTMEG comes from the dried seed of the nutmeg tree, an evergreen tree that also produces mace. Nutmeg is extensively used in baking; it also enhances fruit desserts and complements the flavors of spinach, sweet potato, and squashes, including pumpkin. It may also be an element in curry.

Connecticut is known as the Nutmeg State because in the early nineteenth century, unscrupulous peddlers sold wooden nutmegs to housewives.

"*He's the colour of Nutmeg*
...And the heat of Ginger."**

—William Shakespeare
Henry V (ca. 1599)

ONION, GARLIC, SCALLION, and **CHIVES** are related herbs of the lily family. All of these, especially onion and garlic, are not only among the most ancient of cultivated plants, but are among the most widely used herbs across many cultures. Their uses are too numerous to list, and even the most basic of cooks is usually aware of their many virtues.

Both onions and garlic are highly valued in herbal medicine, believed even today to have absorptive and antiseptic qualities. If you have a cold or flu, eat lots of onion and garlic—if you can't bear them raw, make a broth of them or use them profusely in your cooking. Both onion and garlic are mentioned frequently as aphrodisiacs by numerous volumes, both ancient and modern. The onion was regarded as a symbol of the universe by the ancient Egyptians, and was the subject of vast folklore in many cultures. Garlic was considered by many a powerful charm against evil.

Onion's skin, very thin,
Mild winter's coming in.
Onion's skin, thick and tough,
Coming winter cold and rough.

"Our apothecary's shop is our
garden full of pot-herbs, and our
doctor is a good clove of garlic. "

—Anonymous
"A Deep Snow" (1615)

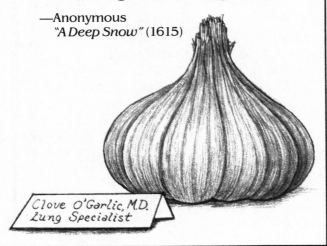

Clove O'Garlic, M.D.
Lung Specialist

PAI'RIKA comes from ground dried sweet red peppers. It enhances cheese and egg dishes, potatoes, and just about all tomato-based dishes. It is also useful as a garnish to give color to the tops of casseroles and such. As widespread as its usage is in cookery, paprika has been virtually ignored by legend and lore.

PARSLEY, one of the most versatile herbs, is common both in flat and curly leaf types. It makes an excellent windowsill herb and I recommend always using it fresh, as it is always available and inexpensive, and has lots of flavor and fragrance, whereas dried parsley has very little. The use of parsley is too extensive to list; there are few categories of cookery, aside from breads and desserts, where it would be unwelcome.

In folklore, it was believed that it was bad luck to cut parsley if one was in love. Certain parsley-lore is interchangeable with cabbage-lore, such as the old English "belief" that babies come from the parsley-bed. Like cabbage, parsley was also believed in ancient Rome to have had the ability to prevent drunkenness, and was thus woven into head-wreaths or worn around the neck. Parsley is a natural breath-sweetener and has numerous nutritive values. For more praise of its virtues, see Parsley Dressing (page 57).

PEPPERCORNS are the small dried berries of an evergreen vine and, in ground form, they are what we know as black pepper. Pepper is one of the most ancient of known spices, and again, its uses are too numerous to list. Along with salt, it is the most basic of all seasonings. Any cook worth his or her "salt" knows that it is best to buy whole peppercorns and grind them in a pepper mill as needed. If you've never done this, the extra pleasant bite and fragrance will surprise you.

I speak severely to my boy,
I beat him when he sneezes;
For he can thoroughly enjoy
The pepper when he pleases.

—Louis Carroll
Alice's Adventures in Wonderland (1865)

POPPY SEEDS are, predictably, the seeds of the poppy flower. They are used for certain baked goods and for garnishing breads, and lend an unusual twist to certain noodle dishes (see Egg Noodles with Red Cabbage, page 101), cabbage dishes, and potatoes.

Poppy seeds were once used for divination by magicians: if they were tossed on burning coals and the smoke lingered about, it was a negative omen, but if the smoke ascended straight to the skies, it foretold good fortune.

ROSEMARY comes from the leaves of a small evergreen shrub and is one of the most distinctly flavored of common herbs. It is most useful in tomato-based dishes, and may also be used in small amounts wherever a mixture of herbs is called for.

Rosemary's most celebrated quality in folklore is that of its symbolism as the herb of remembrance, loyalty and friendship. Students in ancient Greece wore wreaths of rosemary leaves, as it was believed to aid the memory. In some places, rosemary was called "elf-leaf," as it was believed that elves had a special affinity for it; in other places, rosemary was supposed to thrive only for the righteous, or where the woman was head of the household, thus the old proverb: "Where Rosemary flourishes, the lady rules."

"There's Rosemary, that's for remembrance: Pray you, love, remember."

—William Shakespeare
Hamlet (ca. 1600)

SAFFRON is the dried, brightly colored stigmas of the autumn crocus. Saffron has always been valued as much for its brilliant yellow color as for its use as a spice. It is by far the most expensive of common spices, and I call for it only once in the recipes (see Saffron Fruited Rice, page 79). It is used mainly in Far Eastern cookery.

Saffron has a very colorful legacy. In the Arabian Nights, it was said to be so powerful an aphrodisiac that it would cause women to swoon. In parts of the Orient, it was used as a perfume and for painting one's body in order to resemble the Buddha. The herbalists praised its power to produce well-being:

"Saffron rejoyceth the heart, comforteth the stomacke, and procureth sleepe."

—William Vaughn
Directions for Health (1617)

"It is an herb of the Sun and under the Lion... It is said to be more cordial, and exhilarating than any other of the aromatics... it strengthens the stomach, helps digestion, and is good in coughs."

—Nicolas Culpeper

SAGE comes from the leaves of an evergreen shrub. Its strong, spicy flavor goes well with squashes, including pumpkin, certain soups, vegetable and grain dishes. Use it subtly.

Sage's legacy is primarily medicinal; it was known as an herb of longevity, and for its ability to strengthen the brain.

SAVORY refers to two varieties of related herbs, summer and winter savory. Summer savory is more accessible and has a subtler flavor, so that is what I call for in recipes. It is extremely useful wherever a mild herb is needed or where mixed herbs are called for, such as in soups, salads, dressings, vegetable and grain dishes, etc. In addition, it has long been known to have a special affinity with beans, sometimes having been called the "bean herb."

Savory is the legendary plant of the satyrs, as is implied by its latin name, "satureja."

"It maketh thin and doth marvellously prevail against winde: therefore it is with good success boyled and eaten with beans, peason, and other windie pulses . . . "

—John Gerarde
The Herball (1636)

SESAME SEEDS are the seeds of a tropical herbal plant. They are useful in baking and as a garnish for breads, casseroles, Oriental dishes, and salads. They are the basis for tahini (sesame paste), halvah (sesame candy), and sesame oil, which I call for in many of the Oriental-style recipes. Although it is a bit expensive, its flavor and fragrance give Chinese dishes an authentic touch.

Almost everyone has heard the command "Open, Sesame!" from *The Arabian Nights* (see Crisp Sesame Vegetables, page 40), and perhaps because they are packed with vitamin E, sesame seeds are considered by some an aphrodisiac (see Sesame Date Brownies, page 156).

TARRAGON is a perennial Old World plant and is one of the most expensive of herbs, so if I call for it in the recipes, its use is optional. Tarragon has a very distinctive, fresh, sweetish taste. It is well known for its use in tarragon vinegar and it goes well in salads and with green vegetables.

Its name may have come from the Arabic "Tarkum," meaning dragon, perhaps because its roots resemble that fire-breathing beast.

THYME is an aromatic herb of the mint family. It is a widely useful culinary herb with a strong flavor that makes an impression even when used sparingly. It is excellent in soups, gives a nice zest to tomato-based dishes, and goes well with grains, beans, vegetables, and most anywhere a mixture of herbs is called for.

In ancient Greece, one of the greatest compliments was to be told that one smelled of thyme; there and in other places, thyme was a symbol of courage and strength. Elves, fairies and bees were said to have a special love for thyme.

*I know a bank where the wild
	Thyme blows,
Where Oxlips and the woody Violet
	grows,
Quite over-canopied with lush
	Woodbine
With sweet Musk-Roses and with
	Eglantine...*

—William Shakespeare
A Midsummer Night's Dream (ca. 1595)

TURMERIC comes from the underground root of a plant related to ginger. Turmeric is most useful in curries, giving them their fiery yellow color. Use it in small amounts to brighten egg and cheese dishes as well. Its scent is reminiscent of wood, but its flavor is harder to define.

Like saffron, turmeric has long been valued for its color, and in the Far East was used as a cosmetic. In other places, it was burned in order to ward off spirits, and in India, turmeric was an element in wedding rituals and in erotic play.

APPENDIX:
Cooking Notes

COOKING GRAINS

In the recipes, where a specific amount of grains are needed, I give the dry amount in order to eliminate any guesswork. In other instances, where grains are called for to serve as a bed for vegetables, beans, and such, remember that grains swell to approximately two and one-half times their original volume.

BROWN RICE

One nice thing about cooking brown rice is that it doesn't become sticky, due to the fact that the starch is not exposed. Rinse the rice well and place in a pot or heavy saucepan and cover with water in 2½ to 1 ratio. Bring to a boil, then lower heat and simmer, covered (leave the cover a bit ajar so that the steam can escape). Check after 35 minutes. Add a bit more water if need be and simmer another 5 minutes or so uncovered. If there is still unabsorbed water, on the other hand, simply allow it to simmer uncovered until it is absorbed.

WHEAT BERRIES

Rinse the berries and place them in a pot or heavy saucepan and cover with water in a 3 to 1 ratio. Bring to a boil, then lower heat and simmer, covered as described for rice, for 45 to 55 minutes, depending on how chewy you like them. Add more water as needed or drain off any excess when cooked.

BULGUR

Place the amount of bulgur needed in a bowl. Boil water in a 2 to 1 ratio and pour it over the bulgur. Cover and let stand for about 30 minutes. The water should be absorbed; taste to see if the bulgur is done to your liking, remembering that it has a chewy texture. If not, add another ½ cup boiling water, let stand another 10 minutes, then drain off any excess water.

MILLET

In a pot or heavy saucepan, melt a tablespoon of butter or heat a tablespoon of oil, per about 1 cup raw millet. Add the millet and stir quickly over moderate heat until it is coated. Continue to stir for a minute or so. Then follow the instructions exactly as for rice. Millet cooks to a mush texture.

BARLEY

Cook exactly as directed for brown rice, but check the water situation after 25 or 30 minutes, as barley seems to vary in how much it absorbs.

COUSCOUS

Prepare exactly as directed for bulgur; the difference will be that the couscous will be done in only 10 to 15 minutes.

BUCKWHEAT GROATS (KASHA)

First, make sure that whoever you serve this to likes it. People seem to either love or dislike its very distinct flavor. Assuming you are cooking 1 cup raw groats, break an egg into a bowl and beat it well. Mix the groats into the egg until evenly coated. Heat 1 tablespoon of oil in a large skillet and at the same time bring 2 cups of water to a boil separately. Toast the groats in the skillet until the egg is dry and the grains are separated. Pour the boiling water over them, cover, and simmer over low heat for 20 minutes. At this time, check to see if they are done to your liking. If not, add a bit more water and simmer uncovered until it is absorbed. Don't let the groats burst and get mushy.

COOKING BEANS (including lentils)

I give cooked as well as raw amounts for beans in the recipes in order to give the option of using canned beans. Using raw beans is preferable, and besides, a display of them in jars in your kitchen looks very enticing. The rule of thumb is to remember that raw beans swell to 2 1/4 to 2 1/2 times their original bulk when cooked.

To cook kidney, red, navy, great northern or soy beans, chick-peas, or blackeye peas, first wash them well and discard any withered or discolored ones. Place them in a pot or heavy saucepan and cover with water in a 3 to 1 ratio. Bring to a boil, turn off the heat and cover tightly. Soak for 2 hours or so before continuing to cook over low heat until tender. Alternately, simply, wash, sort and soak the beans in tepid water in the 3 to 1 ratio overnight, then cook until tender on low heat.

Red, kidney, and great northern beans all have approximately the same cooking time and may be cooked together if they are to be combined in a recipe. The others take more or less time and should be cooked separately. Once the beans have been soaked they may take anywhere from 45 minutes to 2 hours to cook, depending on the type of bean and length of soaking time. Check occasionally and add more water as needed while they are cooking. Save the broth that is formed to use as soup stock, whether it is a bean soup or not—the broth's flavor is highly concentrated.

Lentils cook quickly enough without being soaked, but you may soak them to cut down a bit on the time. Wash them well and discard the withered or discolored ones. Cover with water in a 3 to 1 ratio, bring to a boil, then lower the heat and simmer until tender, about 40 minutes or so if you didn't soak them. Check after 35 minutes to see how the water level is; add more if necessary. Watch them carefully in the last stages of cooking, as they go from underdone to mushy very quickly.

STEAMED VEGETABLES

When a recipe calls for vegetables to be steamed, there are two ways to do this. The ideal way is to use a steamer, an inexpensive gadget which serves as a basket to hold the vegetables above the simmering water. Fill a large pot with about an inch or so of water, place the steamer in, followed by the vegetables. Cover tightly and simmer over low heat until the vegetables are done to a tender-crisp texture. Stir them once in a while and check to see if there is still enough water in the bottom.

Alternatively, you can heat 1/2 inch (1 1/2 cm) of water in a large pot or skillet, add the vegetables, then cover tightly and simmer, stirring occasionally and adding only enough water to keep the bottom of the pot or skillet moist.

HOW TO FRY AND FLIP A SKILLET PIE OR FRITTATA

The best tool for a successful skillet pie or frittata is an 8-to 10-inch (20 to 25 cm) nonstick, Silverstone-type skillet. Without it, you will have to rely on skill and luck. Heat just enough oil or butter to coat the bottom of the skillet and allow it to get hot over moderate heat. Test with a drop of batter or water and if it really sizzles, it is ready. Pour the contents of the skillet pie or frittata into the skillet. Smooth it out quickly with a wide spatula. Turn to moderately low heat, cover, and fry until the bottom is nicely browned and the top is fairly set.

Tipping the skillet, slide the pie out onto a flat plate. Hold the plate on the bottom, and invert the skillet over the plate. Quickly turn the skillet right side up again, return to heat and remove the plate. Fry uncovered until the second side is nicely browned. In most cases you will cut into wedges to serve.

A WORD ABOUT METRIC CONVERSIONS

The metric conversions given in this book are approximate. Also, standard American weights of certain items such as canned goods are converted to the approximate metric weight. In this case, of course, the closest size can (or whatever item is in question) to the stated metric weight may be used.

SELECTED SOURCES

Barkas, Janet. *The Vegetable Passion* (New York: Charles Scribner's Sons, 1975)

Billings, Josh (Henry Wheeler Shaw). *His Works, Complete* (New York: G.W. Carleton & Co., 1876)

Billings, Josh. *Josh Billings' Farmer's Alminax* (New York: G.W. Carleton & Co., 1870–1873)

Boorde, Dr. Andrew. *A Compendyous Regyment or a Dyetary of Healthe* (London: W. Powell, 1567)

Botlan, Ibn. *Tacuinum Sanitatis—The Medieval Health Handbook,* translated by Luisa Cogliata Arano (New York: George Brazillier, 1976)

Brody, Rosalie. *Emily Post Weddings* (New York: Simon & Schuster, 1963)

Butler, Samuel. *Erewhon* (New York: Penguin Books, 1970 printing of 1872 edition)

Carroll, Lewis. *Alice's Adventures in Wonderland* (London; 1865)

Carroll, Lewis. *Through the Looking Glass* (London; 1871)

Carson, Gerald. *Cornflake Crusade* (New York: Rinehart & Co., 1957)

Chesterton, G.K. *The Collected Poems of G.K. Chesterton* (New York: Dodd, Mead & Co., 1911)

Culpeper, Nicolas. *Culpeper's Complete Herbal* (London: Reprinted by Foulsham Co., undated)

Daniels, Cora Linn. *Encyclopedia of Superstitions, Folklore, and the Occult Sciences* (Detroit: Gale Research Co., 1971 reprint of 1803 edition)

Edwards, E.D. *The Dragon Book* (London: William Hodge & Co., 1938)

Ellacombe, Henry N. *The Plant-Lore and Gardencraft of Shakespeare* (London: Edward Arnold Publishers, 1896)

Evelyn, John. *Acetaraia: A Discourse of Sallets* (London: 1699)

Folkard, Richard. *Plant-Lore, Legends and Lyrics* (London: S. Lowe Marston, Serale, & Rivington, 1884)

Ford, Paul Leicester. *The Many Sided Franklin* (New York: Books for Libraries Press, 1972 reprint of 1898 edition)

Franklin, Benjamin. *Poor Richard's Almanack* (New York: Peter Pauper Press, undated reprint of 1734 edition)

Frazer, Sir James George. *The Golden Bough* (New York: MacMillan, 1948)

Friedman, Margaret B. *Herbs for the Medieval Household* (New York: The Metropolitan Museum, 1943)

Fuller, Edmund, ed. *Voltaire, a Reader* (New York: Dell Publishing, 1959)

Gerarde, John. *The Herball or General Historie of Plantes* (London: 1636)

Giehl, Dudley. *Vegetarianism, A Way of Life* (New York: Barnes and Noble Books, 1979)

Hardy, Thomas. *Jude the Obscure* (New York: New American Library, 1961 reprint of 1885 edition)

Hawthorne, Nathaniel. *The Scarlet Letter* (New York: Random House, 1950 printing of 1850 edition)

Hayman, Ronald. *Kafka* (London: Oxford University Press, 1981)

Hubbard, Alice, and Babbitt, Adeline, eds. *The Golden Flute* (New York: The John Day Co., 1932)

Jones, Evan. *A Food Lover's Companion* (New York: Harper and Row, 1979)

Jones, Frederick C. *Letters of Percy Bysshe Shelley* (Oxford: Clarendon Press, 1964)

Klaw, Spencer. *Horizon* Magazine, Spring 1976, Volume XVIII #2, "Pursuing Health in the Promised Land"

Kronenberger, Louis. *Animal Vegetable Mineral* (New York: Viking Press, 1975)

Leach, Maria, ed. *Funk & Wagnalls Standard Dictionary of Folklore, Mythology, and Legend,* Vols. 1 and 2 (New York: Funk & Wagnalls, div. of Readers Digest Books, 1949)

Lehner, Ernst and Johanna. *Folklore and Odysseys of Food and Medicinal Plants* (New York: Farrar Straus Giroux, 1962)

Leibman, Malvina W. *From Caravan to Casserole* (Miami: E.A. Seeman Publishing, 1977)

Lorwin, Madge. *Dining with William Shakespeare* (New York: Atheneum, 1976)

Mencken, H.L. *A New Dictionary of Quotations* (New York: Alfred A. Knopf, 1966)

National Pasta Association
P.O. Box 1008
Palatine, Illinois 60067

Nefzawi, Shaykh. *The Perfumed Garden,* translated by Sir Richard Burton (St. Albans, England: Granada Publishing, 1963 reprint of 1876 edition)

Northcote, Lady Rosalind. *The Book of Herb-Lore* (New York: Dover Publishing, 1971 reprint of 1812 edition)

Opie, Iona and Peter, eds. *The Oxford Dictionary of Nursery Rhymes* (New York: Oxford University Press, 1952)

Parker, Dorothy. *The Wonderful World of Yogurt* (New York: Hawthorne Books, 1972)

Paul, Anita May, and Kotlatch, David, ed. *Completely Cheese—The Cheese Lover's Companion* (New York: Jonathan David Publishers, 1975)

Penner, Lucille Recht. *The Colonial Cookbook* (New York: Hastings House, 1976)

Prezzolini, Giuseppe. *Spaghetti Dinner—A History of Spaghetti and Cooking* (New York: Abelard-Shulman, 1955)

Prochnow, Herbert V. *A Treasury of Humorous Quotations* (New York: Harper and Row, 1969)

Rhind, William. *A History of the Vegetable Kingdom* (Glasgow: Blackie & Son, 1870)

Rosegarten, Frederick Jr. *The Book of Spices* (New York: Pyramid Books, 1973)

Spence, Lewis. *An Encyclopedia of Occultism* (New Hyde Park, NY: University Books, 1968)

Stevenson, Burton, ed. *The Macmillan Book of Proverbs, Maxims, and Famous Phrases* (New York: MacMillan Co., 1948)

Thackeray, William Makepeace. *Vanity Fair* (New York: Dell Publishing, 1961 printing of 1848 edition)

Thoreau, Henry David. *Walden* (New York: New American Library, 1962 reprint of 1854 edition)

Trager, James. *Foodbook* (New York: Grossman Publishers, 1970)

Twain, Mark (Samuel L. Clemens). *A Tramp Abroad* (Hartford: American Publishing Co., Hartford)

Twain, Mark. *Pudd'nhead Wilson* (New York: New American Library, 1964 printing of 1894 edition)

Vatsyayana. *The Kama Sutra of Vatsyayana—A New Translation* (New Hyde Park, NY: University Books, 1968)

Vaughn, William. *Naturall and Artificiall Directions for Health* (London, 1600)

Vaughn, William. *Directions for Health, both Naturall and Artificiall* (London, 1617)

Verrill, Hyatt. *Foods America Gave the World* (Boston: L.C. Page and Co., 1937)

Williams, Harold, ed. *The Poems of Jonathan Swift* (London: Oxford University Press, 1966)

Winston, Stephen. *Shaw's Corner* (New York: Roy Publishers, 1952)

Yutang, Lin. *My Country and My People* (New York: John Day Co., 1938)

INDEX

NOTES

NOTES

NOTES

NOTES

This book is set in ITC Benguiat,
designed for the International Typeface
Corporation by Ed Benguiat.

Composition by Scarlett Letters, Inc.,
New York City.